Gumption

Get up & go !
Faye

Gumption

Faye Berger

NORTH STAR PRESS OF ST. CLOUD, INC.

St. Cloud, Minnesota

Photo on the title page:
The Gang: Russ, Wilbur, Donnie, Elmer, Hubert.

Copyright © 2010 Faye Berger

ISBN: 978-0-87839-404-3

Printed in the United States of America

Published by
North Star Press of St. Cloud, Inc.
P.O. 451
St. Cloud, Minnesota 56302

northstarpress.com

In memory of Russel E. Albrecht
(that's Russel with one "l")

*"Age is strictly a case of mind over matter.
If you won't mind, it doesn't matter.
Jack Benny*

Acknowledgments

First and foremost, to my husband: Thank you, Wilt, for your endless encouragement, support, enthusiasm, and patience, for your loving advice, and for always being there when I needed to print a simple label.

To my sisters who wondered just what I was up to during that long time of writing and then got behind my project with gusto.

To my children who can't get enough of Grandpa's stories.

To the Morgan community that inspired me, especially the trusting families who were part of this story.

To the Morgan teachers who encouraged me always to reach high—Mrs. Lange, Mrs. Valle, Mr. Wittgraf, Mr. Knowles.

To The Loft Literary Center with its outstanding instructors.

To Marion, Judith, Molly, Deb, Diane - for giving me feedback

To North Star Press for seeing the importance of a story on aging.

To dear friend and indomitable George who died this year at age 95, for his instruction, "Get your book done!"

And finally, to all my most senior friends, whether living unassisted or in nursing homes, who continue to amaze me with their gumption.

FOREWORD

Stories about the Gang were told to me by my dad. Always a colorful storyteller, he liked an audience, and he wasn't a bit shy in giving his opinion. Like listening to the latest adventures on a radio serial, I was caught up in the drama of it all and too, so inspired by the resiliency and resourcefulness of these gentlemen.

It wasn't until after Dad's death in 2003 that I became intrigued with the notion of capturing these stories in book form. I interviewed the one remaining member of the Gang and the adult children of the others, including my two sisters. My other research included topics as diverse as the Thirtieth Division Infantry battles and Carnival Cruise ship amenities.

And like any story telling, I have taken liberties with creating dialogue, actions, and circumstances. If I have misrepresented in any way, I apologize. The story is set in the years 1986 to 1996. For many of the characters, I've changed the names. The actual names I've used are: Russel Albrecht, Lorraine Albrecht, Roy Hanson, Richard Frederiksen, Elmer Bendixen, Hubert Iffert, Donnie Koblin, Wilbur Best, Agnes Ziegenhagen, Hollis "Red" Degenhardt, and Clarence E. Dale. God bless them all.

TABLE OF CONTENTS

Chapter 1
Winter Weather Advisory

Th"hat's the latest on the weather, folks—looks like a blustery, snowy night ahead. Be sure to tune in at five o'clock tomorrow morning for the list of school closings." Russ clicked the TV remote and switched off the lamp as he got up from his recliner and headed for the kitchen to turn out the last light in the house before going to bed. With the house dark, he looked out the kitchen window and saw snow accumulating in a drift around the back steps, the way it always did when wind mixed with a good snowfall. *Not much there yet but wait until morning*, he predicted to himself. Looking off to the streetlight at the end of the block, he could see the sheets of falling snow swirling down, dancing almost, as if on stage under the light on the empty road. "Yeah, this could amount to something," he murmured with a look of satisfaction true to an old Minnesotan, then closed the curtain and headed off to bed.

Just fifteen minutes later—as Russ settled under the covers in his bed drifting off, feeling particularly cozy and comfortable and lulled by the rhythm of the furnace creaking inside and the wind gusting outside—the telephone rang. It was shrill and jolting in the darkness. Russ fumbled with the light and reached for the receiver on the bedstand.

"Yeah?"

"Hello. Is this Mr. Albrecht, Russel E. Albrecht?"

"Yes it is. But hold on just a minute . . ." Russ grabbed his hearing aid and adjusted it in his ear with his free hand. He leaned up on his elbow holding the receiver out a bit from his ear until the hearing aid was firmly in place. "Now I can hear you better. Okay, now you can talk."

"Yes, Mr. Albrecht. Hello, and sorry for calling at this late hour. This is the medical monitoring center for Richard Frederiksen. He has activated his personal help system."

"You say Rich's in trouble?"

"He activated the system, which means he needs help in some way, yes. Please check on his condition, assess the situation, and let us know if you need further assistance. Just hit the big red button on his telephone labeled 'monitoring center.' My name is Ann, and I'll be standing by to hear back from you, Mr. Albrecht. Just remember to look for the red button."

Richard Frederiksen.

"Sure, sure," Russ was sitting up now and grabbing for his clothes and shoes as he cradled the receiver on his shoulder. "I'll hightail it right over there." Without another word, he hung up the receiver. His hands shook as he dressed, his breathing coming fast and shallow.

"What the heck's going on, Rich? Just hang on, buddy."

With shirt-tail half out of his pants, he zipped his jacket, grabbed his cap and gloves and headed out the back door. Halfway down the steps deep in snow he wished he'd remembered his overshoes, but with no time to waste, he didn't turn back. The wind and snow whipped around his neck. He pulled his collar up and hunched his shoulders to his ears as he cautiously side-stepped the drifted snow and headed to the garage, unprotected from the bitter northwest wind. Another drift was forming in its usual pattern encircling the little garage.

The cold car seat sent a shiver up his back, even with his extra layer of thermal long underwear. As grace would have it that blustery night, just one turn of the ignition was all it took to get the motor raring to go. With a firm foot on the accelerator, Russ revved the motor, shifted to reverse, and rammed the car over the drift. He felt a thud on the muffler and tailpipe as the underbelly hit the drift and another thud with the drift at the curb. With a quick turn of the wheels, he came to a stop in the middle of the blanketed, empty street. He turned the windshield wipers and defrost fan on high as he hunched up close over the steering wheel to make out what was ahead. He peered over his fogged-up glasses through the small clearing in the windshield.

"Whew . . ." His breath formed a cloud. "Just hang on, Rich. I'm on my way." Russ shifted into drive and eased the car forward, feeling the tires grab the snow, then slowly gaining momentum, he headed to the main highway from the west, just two blocks away. The stiff car lumbered like a tank. The highway was deserted, stretching out into the darkness of farmland on the edge of town. Only the drifting snow scurried over the blacktop. Russ saw the empty road as his opportunity to ignore the stop sign and actually to speed through and into the turn. Otherwise, he would risk getting stuck— seventy years of Minnesota winter driving had taught him that.

After maneuvering the turn in fine form and now out alone on the highway at the city limits of Morgan, Russ realized that the town was still, except for the street signs shimmying in the wind. *Like a winter ghost town*, he thought as he drove past the grain elevators projecting like dark skyscrapers in the prairie town. Apparently all 975-or-so Morgan residents were hunkered in their homes at that hour, except for the clerk at the Texaco station who had his nose in a *Popular Mechanics* so he didn't notice the single car out on the road, and the new town cop who was parked on Vernon Avenue near the intersection, half dozing as he watched for anyone who might think they could speed through Morgan unnoticed, even on a wintry night such as this. Russ gave him a nod.

Just two blocks past the intersection, Russ turned to the south road, then just past the remodeled mortuary he turned on to a street of newer homes, then into Rich's driveway. As he turned off the ignition, he took a deep breath and blew the air out slowly through pursed lips, a useful trick to get more air in his lungs. His heart raced.

Rich's house was dark, like all the other houses on the block with most everyone in bed at that hour. The only streetlight was three houses away, but with snow illuminating the ground, Russ found his way to the familiar back door. He kicked away the snow drifted up against the storm door so that he could open it to get at the lock of the inside door.

"Rich!" he hollered. "It's Russ. Where are you, Rich?" He fumbled for the light switch on the wall in the entry as he stomped off the snow. Then, he turned to listen with his good ear.

"Russel! Russel!" It was Rich's faint voice from several rooms away. "I'm here . . . here by the TV . . ."

"Yeah, okay!" Russ didn't bother with his jacket but just headed in the direction of Rich's voice.

"I'd be there to greet you formally, but well . . . you'll see. Say, what took you so long, my friend? Did you go back to sleep?"

Russ heard a weak chuckle, followed by a groan. He hurried through the kitchen and towards the living room, turning on lights as he went. At the living room, he stopped short, seeing two legs flat on the floor jutting from behind the recliner. "Oh, oh." Russ scrambled for the lamp switch, careful to step over the big slippered feet pointing straight up like cones on the highway marking a danger zone. "*What do we have here* . . . ?" His voice trailed in disbelief as he looked down at Rich in the light now, sprawled out on the floor, all six feet, 175 pounds of him. "Holy smokes, Rich! Where're you hurt? Don't move!"

Rich squinted from the light. "No, no, Russel, nothing like that. I'm not hurt—just can't get up, that's all! Nothing to grab hold of!" Exasperated, he swooped his long arms out in all directions to prove his point.

"But I heard you groan. What's that all about? Must be something hurt?"

"No, I tell you, Russel, it's just the hard floor and that's the honest truth." He looked at his watch. "Been here a bit, you know, and these old bones are complaining. Tell you what, Russel, I'd prefer my soft bed. Yes, sir, my bed would be nice." He waited for a reaction but then thought better of it. "I never did like tenting—laying on a hard ground all night, and that's what this is like, hard ground." He pounded his fist into the carpet. "Well, sort of like hard ground." His eyes lit up with a familiar twinkle. He never tired of joking. But Russ, now in his new role as rescuer, was not amused. He shook his head like a stern adult not entertained by childish pranks.

"Oh, come on now, Russ, you have to admit it *is* pretty funny—us old guys in this situation. We need one of those hoists from the body shop to get this body of mine up, don't you think, huh?"

"Yeah, yeah, maybe joking isn't such a bad idea, Rich, but you darned well better not be making that up—you know, the part about you not being hurt." He cast an even sterner look straight into Rich's eyes.

"It's the honest truth, Russel. I'm just stuck here on the floor, that's all. Stuck!"

Russ backed off. "Well, guess I have to agree with you then, Richard, the bed is definitely a better place to sleep, where, you know, *regular* folks like to curl up and not sprawled out like you here." Russ forced a grin. Joking around wasn't exactly his inclination at this moment, given the emergency situation, and after all, this was the middle of the night, he had been roused out of bed, and his friend was on the floor—nothing funny about that. Russ felt more in the mood to lecture, so he did. "Just look at you, Richard! It's a good thing you didn't hit your noggin and knock yourself out, have one of those concussions, or even worse—break a hip! That's what happens to old duffers like us. Hell, that's the next thing to checking into a nursing home! You're smart enough to know that! And after a guy is in the home, well, you know what's next . . . you'll be in a wheelchair the rest of your life, whether you can walk or not. Then pretty soon a nurse with a wide behind will be helping you in the can. Maybe you won't even know your name anymore! And someone will be spooning mush in your mouth!" He took a breath and paused just long enough to notice Rich's hurt expression, a look of boyish innocence and helpless old man. Rich stared up at Russ, waiting for him to finish. Meanwhile, Russ felt like giving himself a punch to the old melon, seeing that face, which could easily have been his own. Even to mention a nursing home, well, that kind of threat was a bit too harsh to say to someone like Richard Frederiksen, who was in fact a model of senior independence. Rich preached it in fact, knowing firsthand the stark realities of sickness and old age. Cancer in all its glory—that's what Rich knew. He, of all people, didn't need to be hollered at. After all, that's what this medical monitoring was all about—independence.

Russ unclenched his jaw. He cleared his throat and took a deep breath to ease into a more productive approach. "Now, tell me, Richard, how in the heck did you get yourself in this predicament anyway?" He took off his jacket and cap and threw them in the easy chair.

Rich's tense face eased into a gentle smile, but still with a hesitant raised brow to be certain that Russ had said his piece. "Ahh, yeah . . . well, I was just heading to bed, my friend. I turned the light out, got up from my chair, and lost my balance, that's all, Russel. Should have done it more slowly, I guess. My feet got all tangled up, and down I tumbled. I missed the coffee table anyway!" He grinned as he motioned to the sharp corner of the table. "I tried to roll over so I could crawl to the wall and prop myself up—but no use. This big belly of mine doesn't help matters." He patted his middle with a sigh.

It was true. The physics of getting Rich up presented a problem. Even after two surgeries, the huge tumor in his stomach was noticeable, especially for an otherwise slim man. Russ stood there with arms folded and one hand under his chin, running some figures through his head. At five feet, five inches and weighing in at just under 120 pounds, he might have to perform a small miracle to assist his friend to his feet. And then who's to say he'd stay up? They could both come tumbling down for that matter and then that emergency crew would have *double* duty—and that's if either one could actually get to the phone to call! Russ was sure that no one explained this sort of scenario when he agreed to the arrangement with the medical monitoring company.

"Okay, Rich, here's what I need to do: I just need to get on this special phone of yours to get some help. For heaven's sakes, that's what it's here for—let's get the professionals!" Russ wondered why he got sidetracked in the first place and didn't march to the telephone right off the bat. Thrilled with this revelation, his mood brightened considerably. "Let's see, the gal said to look for a red button. In fact, they will probably be calling here in a few minutes—oh, my gosh, I'd better hurry." He looked at his watch and started for the phone.

"No, Russel! No! We can do this ourselves!" Adamant now, Rich waved his arms like he was stopping traffic. "I don't want an ambulance here with all that commotion and expense. I can picture it: The whole family would be here. My daughter would be calling, and even the grandkids, the whole bunch, would be driving in from all over the place and staying for days. And just because I tumbled down."

"But . . ."

"No, now just let me finish, Russel. Everyone tumbles down at one time or another. You said so yourself." He pointed an accusing finger to Russ. "Hey, remember that fall you had at Wally's Garage right smack into the grease pit when you weren't looking? Bruises and everything, but you just jumped right out of there and went on with your business, didn't you? Huh?"

Russ had his head cocked slightly wondering how that story had any similarity whatsoever to Rich's *not* jumping up and getting on with his business.

Rich didn't wait for an answer. "I can see it now, even that nosy new Morgan cop will show up. Then they'll be talking about it at the pool hall. And then pretty soon I *will* be in the nursing home! Don't you see? I just can't get *up*, that's all! Tell you what, Russel: If I have anything ailing me when you get me up, *anything whatsoever,* I *promise* to see a doctor. Let's at least give it a try, Russel. Please! That's the reason I named *you* on this deal—I knew I could trust you not to raise a big fuss. Think about it, Russel. *TRUST!*" Rich threw up his arms in one last desperate appeal and then dropped them to his sides, thumping in a theatrical sort of way as they hit the carpet.

"Hmm." That use of the word "trust" wasn't really fair, Russ thought looking down at his pajamaed friend, raising such a fuss and looking so pathetic stranded there on the floor. Using a word like "trust" was sort of like saving up a trump card, but in this case a real-life winning trick that might save a guy from the sentence of, say, a nursing home, to be perfectly honest about it. The drama of it all caught him off guard too. Rich was always good with drama. Good enough in fact that Russ stopped short of his mission to get to that red button. Now with his hand resting on the phone, his mind raced back to his own fall a few years ago in Wally's grease pit, then to this present dilemma with his buddy throwing out this word "trust" right here in the middle of an emergency situation, leaving not much time for a guy to consider all the sides to such a serious word as "trust."

It's true that he and Rich had hit it off in a sort of odd way the past six years after they both became widowers, certainly not planned or predicted, but as Russ would say, they were "darned good pals when it got down to it." They came to rely on each other, which he'd have to admit, was about the same as trust. They didn't have much in common really with the roads they had traveled, yet both had the knack for so-cializing and a knack for casting a positive spin on almost anything life could dish out. "Survivors" was how he heard Oprah describe this kind of attitude that he and Rich seemed to have. Too, they had some-thing else in common, a skill not shared by many of the men in the small farming community: each could find his way around a kitchen, given the need. Considering this need surfacing now late in life after being fed and catered to by doting wives for some forty years, cooking was no small accomplishment. "We can figure this out—we can get our own grub," Russ liked to boast when he and Rich teamed up in the kitchen. Remembering that now while looking at Rich flat on the floor, it seemed a stretch of the imagination. But then, after all, anyone can stumble and fall. He pictured the grease pit.

"Trust, you say . . . hmm." Russ hemmed and hawed, then lifted his hand from the phone and turned back to face Rich. "Well, I guess you really aren't hurt by the looks of it. So, okay, let's see what happens, but we've got to hurry up before that gal calls. Here, give me your hand, and I'll get you sitting up anyway."

Relieved, Rich closed his eyes with that generous smile. "Thank you, Lord, for Russel."

"Well, let's get going, and we'll thank the Lord directly, here in a minute."

Rich's eyes popped open, and he reached for Russ' hand. Still hesitant about moving this lug of a body, Russ pulled gently, half-expecting a more vigorous attempt from Rich, who only managed to lift his head. His body might as well have been a gunnysack of dirt, Russ muddled, for the lack of help. "Well, okay, that didn't work. Let's see . . ." Russ looked to make sure he had enough working room behind him. "Let's try this again, but with some *muscle* this time. And don't let go, whatever you do!"

At full attention, Rich nodded a quick okay.

"So, I'll count to three. Then up." Russ planted his feet and used a double grip on Rich's hand. "One . . . two . . . three . . . UP!" Almost losing his balance as he leaned back, Russ pulled Rich forward just enough that he could swing his arm behind to hold himself. He let go of Russ's hand, then dropped that arm back, with his long frame now in more or less a crab position, an unsteady one at that.

Infuriated with his own limitations, not to mention Rich's failing body, Russ barked, "Naw, naw, this is no good! You look wobbly as heck, plus I can't budge you any more than what I just did. We're not exactly the same size, you know!" He was breathing fast again, shaking his head as he wiped his brow, his head buzzing. "You'd better get back down again and let's do something else . . . exactly *what*, I don't know. I'll have to think a minute. Here, I'll put this pillow down, and you can ease on to it." Russ grabbed Rich's hand again and lowered him to the pillow.

"Well now, this pillow is an improvement, that's for sure. Feels almost like bed, my friend. Thanks." Rich looked exhausted and content to lie there, pleased somehow for the camaraderie, even though his friend was in a foul mood. "Say, Russel, did I ever tell you why Danes never play hide and seek?" He stared up at the ceiling with a sly grin, twiddling his fingers on his chest, waiting for Russ' response.

Russ was surveying the room, eyeing all the possibilities for leveraging a 175-pound man. "Huh? Hide and seek? What are you talking about? Is this another one of your jokes?"

"Yeah, as a matter of a fact, it is." Rich waited again but only long enough to see that Russ wasn't going to fall for it. "Okay, then, I'll tell you: Danish people never play hide and seek b-e-c-a-u-s-e . . ." Rich always liked to ham up the punch line, so he stretched out his arms and flicked his wrists as if to a drum roll, ". . . NOBODY wants to look for them!" He began to snicker even before the punch line, and then he broke out into a full belly laugh, jiggling that big torso.

Russ just raised his eyebrows and shook his head, still not amused. He was the one on the hot seat after all. He was the one who was responsible and who, so far at least, hadn't accomplished the job. Hell, at such a critical time as this, that's when emergency people ought to be called, people trained for this kind of situation and not just another old duffer, especially when he's only half the size of the guy in trouble! All this was racing through his mind as he eyed the room for a solution. But Rich's humor was like a dose of brandy warming his insides, trickling down, down, so that he couldn't help but grin like somehow his mouth was wired to the warm feeling inside. And, seeing his friend in those big orange knit slippers with bony white ankles and in his rumpled pajamas buttoned one button off and imprinted with Twins Baseball insignias, which now, it seemed, were bouncing around with the giggling—well, that was funny. Russ tried to hold back but couldn't resist the old Dane's charm. The laughter smoothed his jagged nerves.

"Richard, tell me, how is it that you have a joke for every occasion, huh? Do you have a book of jokes or what? And, by the way, where in hell did you find those Twins pajamas, anyway?"

"I thought you'd enjoy that one, Russel, considering you might have had that very thought, getting out on a night like this to help an old Dane like myself." He looked at his sleeve. "Oh, yeah, these pajamas were a present from my grandson after the Twins won the Series in '87. Nice, huh?"

The telephone startled the two with a shrill *rring-rring*! "H-o-l-y smokes! That's louder than mine!" Russ scampered over Rich like a scared rabbit to answer the phone on the lamp table. He took a deep breath and blew out slowly and waited for another ring. He sing-songed, "Bet I know who it is too-oo . . ." He raised and cocked his eyebrows back at Rich conveying a message something like: "Okay, this is it. I'm going to ask for assistance just like I was told." Actually, he considered that option again now that the opportunity was presenting itself, but all he really intended to do was to return some of the drama that Rich was dishing out.

Rich nervously motioned to Russ and whispered as if the caller could already hear, "You tell them I'm just fine, and we don't need their help. Russel, you tell them. P-l-e-a-s-e . . ."

As Russ picked up the receiver, he kept his eyes on Rich there on the floor frantically waving his hands and shaking his head in a firm "NO!" Russ cleared his throat and answered, nodding back at Rich when he heard the woman's voice that, yes, this was the follow-up call.

Rich's eyes pleaded. His whisper was loud now as well and enunciated for lip-reading, "T-r-u-s-t!" A spec of saliva punctuated the plea.

Russ paused, rationalizing his plan again to himself while watching his friend's antics as a backdrop on the floor. He cleared his throat for more time. Then, with mind made up, he reported to the other end of the line, in his most matter-of-fact, in-control, first-call-response kind of voice, "Thanks, miss, but no further help will be required." After the words came out, he couldn't help but gulp, feeling his throat tighten in a frightening grip. This was like letting go of a life raft to swim for shore, and with minimal swimming skills at best! His heart was pounding at his eardrums. He glared at Rich who was wide-eyed now in anticipation, with his head half raised off the floor. That glare was easy enough for Rich to interpret too. It meant something like: "Okay, buddy, I'm coming through for you, but this better work, or else!"

Turning back to the receiver and in an extra-polite tone, Russ continued, "Yes, miss, Richard is doing just fine. He just couldn't get up, but everything is under control now. I'll be heading back to my house in just a few minutes. In fact, I was just about to head out now—we've got a good little snowstorm going, you know. What's that? You say you want to talk with him?" Russ' eyes were wide as he took a split second to sum up the length of the phone cord and approximate the distance between him and Rich. "Well, ah . . . sure . . . here he is sitting on the edge of his bed as good as ever! Hold on just a minute . . ." Russ raised his eyebrows at Rich again and stretched the phone cord as far as it would go which happened to be just enough to reach Rich's long out-stretched fingers.

Russ rolled his eyes, and Rich crinkled his nose in a confident grin. He cleared his throat. "Yes, m'am, Richard Frederiksen here." His voice came across like a slick salesman. "My good friend, Russel, boosted me up just right. I had a little fall on the carpet but I didn't get hurt—just couldn't get up by myself, that's all. I'm just fine now, in fact getting ready for bed." He faked a yawn. "Thank you very much for your fine service though. This here medallion of yours works just great." Listening, he nodded in agreement and grinned as he twiddled the chain around his neck. "Oh, you bet. I'll keep it on at all times. Ah, huh, yes. I sure will. And you have a good night too. Sure was nice talking to you. Bye, bye now." He handed the receiver back to Russ with a mischievous grin, with a finger raised to his lips in a "Shhh."

Russ hung up the phone. He took a deep breath, put his hands on his hips, and began slowly to circle the room. "Ok, Richard. How did that joke go again? No one wants to look for stubborn old Danes, huh? *Stubborn?*"

Rich burst into a giddy laugh as he relaxed back into his pillow. He sighed with contentment and smiled up at the ceiling. "Yup, I'm stubborn for sure."

"Well, just so you know, I came up with an idea just *before* the phone rang. Tell me what you think . . ." Russ, enthused now and re-lieved of the telephone drama, headed for the straight-back chair he had spotted at the desk and brought it up close to Rich. "Okay, here's how it'll go: I figure if you roll on your side and I can push enough, we can get you up on your hands and knees. Then I'll get this chair situated just right so it's in front of you. Then you can grab onto it while I hold it steady. How's that for a plan? I figure it might just work!" He adjusted the chair until it was just so, whistling under his breath in the process.

Rich had been holding his breath just in keeping up with this sudden change of attitude. But he knew that the whistle was a good sign. "Well, Russel, you're the boss. Just tell me what to do. You say to roll over on my side, and you're going to push?" He practiced by rocking his torso.

"That's right. We'll get you on your hands and knees."

Rich continued to roll back and forth, building a momentum. Then with an extra oomph, he swung his arm over with a flop to land on his side. "Praise the Lord," he gasped.

"Okay, okay, Richard . . . that's good! Just hold it now!" Russ clapped as he dashed to the other side of Rich. "Let's see here . . ." He kneeled with his hands on Rich's back. "Now, at the count of three, you roll, and I'll push. We've got to do this together, or it won't work. Remember to get your knees under you at the same time. Okay?"

Rich looked over his shoulder at Russ. "Okay!"

Russ took a deep breath. "Okay now, I'm going to count to three, and then I'll say 'over.' That's when you roll up on your knees.

Rich nodded.

"Okay: One . . . two . . . three . . . OVER!"

Like Jesus himself was down there on the floor with the two of them, the move was something of a miracle! Rich now hunched over and resting on his elbows had his knees under him.

"Good! Now just get up on your hands." Russ steadied him with a hand on his back as Rich straightened his arms. Rich looked up over his glasses at Russ with a proud grin.

Russ adjusted the chair again. "Now, as soon as we get our breath, we'll finish it up. I'll hold tight on this chair so it doesn't move, and you grab here on each side to steady yourself." He let out a long breath.

"Okay, Russel. You're the boss." Rich grunted and grabbed hold of the chair with each hand, his arms trembling. He looked over his glasses again and acknowledged the go-ahead with a wink.

"Now you just need to get one foot under you and lift yourself up, then the other foot. Ready? Take it really slow though . . . s-l-o-w."

Rich just nodded, his head straight ahead, centered with the chair, determined. He lifted his leg in slow motion, balancing with his other knee and keeping a firm grip on the chair. Russ held his breath as he watched the gangly motion, then let out an exaggerated "*whew*" when Rich had both feet firmly planted. Still bent over gripping the sides of the chair, Rich steadied himself. Then, with Russ clutching his forearm, Rich straightened up inch by inch, unfolding his body. Now towering over Russ, he looked down at him with a proud grin as wide as his face, impish with his ruddy cheeks and rumpled white hair. As if he had just completed a high-wire act, with arm outstretched to acknowledge the crowd, he bowed to a make-believe audience. "How about that? We did it, Russel, my friend! I told you! We're a team!"

"Yeah, Richard, we're a team!" Russ was surprised by the tightness in his throat again.

The two old men celebrated their victory with a handshake, and Rich demonstrated his balance with a strut around the room, slow but confident and brushing aside Russ' hand to steady him. "Okay, okay, I believe you. Now get ready for bed, and I'll watch some of the Carson show here in your chair. I'm not leaving until I hear you snoring. And for Pete's sake, keep that medallion thing around your neck in case you need to push the button again. And, don't be shy about pushing it again, damn it! I'll be back at my usual time in the morning, and you darn well better not be on the floor again." He grinned to himself as he watched Rich take off those orange slippers and then slide between the sheets in his Twins pajamas.

"Yeah, yah, you're the boss, Russel, my friend." Rich yawned and closed his eyes.

That's the way it went that late stormy winter night for the two old men. Russ finally pulled the door shut behind him and stepped out into the swirling blizzard again just after midnight. His earlier tracks were now covered, and a drift had formed around the car's back tires. Again with a firm foot on the gas pedal, he maneuvered a quick reverse out of the driveway and then carefully crept his way back home in low gear on the thick snowy streets. It struck him as odd that tonight the wind's howl sounded like someone calling in the darkness. He shivered.

He was sleeping on his good ear so he didn't hear his usual 6:30 alarm and woke only from the bright light streaming in the bedroom window almost an hour and a half later. He propped himself up to see out the window, thoughts of last night coming together, bit by bit, now seeing drifts beautifully sculpted in the yard near the little evergreen tree. The sky was bright blue now and he could hear a snowplow rumbling down the street. "Holy smokes!" In a rush, he dressed, downed his coffee, and headed out to the garage to find a shovel. Clearing the heavy bank across the driveway left by the snowplow was always the toughest shoveling, but Russ tackled it with one goal in mind—this day of all days he needed his car. After four scoops off the shovel, he rested for four long breaths, repeating this until the driveway was just clear enough for the Ford Taurus to slip through.

He skimmed through his daily posting of sales and debits at the Texaco station, completing his work in less than two hours, not the usual two and a half he clocked daily the last ten years after he sold his small grocery store. That's when the big chains forced him out. But on the bright side, which was his usual take even on a life-changing event such as this, his fill-in job now with its few hours a day was just right to supplement his monthly check from Uncle Sam and just right to manage his nervous energy after a lifetime of accountability. Today, as he tallied and balanced the numbers, he acknowledged that the Good Lord was there with a helping hand, so that on a critical morning like this, he could be on his way. And, too, when he left the station, he wondered in amazement at the most unusual efficiency of the snowplow crew that already by mid-morning had cleared most of Morgan's streets and opened a clear shot to Rich's house. The compacted snow crunched as Russ's Ford Taurus traveled the familiar route, almost speeding.

This time at Rich's door, Russ didn't reach for his key—he knocked. Granted, it was a test, but even more so, Russ figured it was the least he could do for a friend's self-respect. He clinked the change in his pocket as he waited. He knocked again, but this time louder. Just as he was ready to knock a third time, Rich's face appeared in the door window with that big familiar smile. The door opened wide. "Russel, my friend, good buddy. Look at me—I'm on my own two feet and not on the floor this time! And, not in my pajamas! Come in, come in."

This was the true Rich, animated, filling the room with energy! Russ took a deep breath and smiled back. "I've got to say, Rich, it's a relief to see you up and around. You sure look like yourself again. Yes, sir!"

"Well, Russ, a person can hardly get through life without falling down, you know!" Rich couldn't have looked much better, Russ thought, standing there good as new in his corduroys and flannel shirt, hair slicked back, and movie star grin. Such a dramatic change could make a guy wonder if last night even happened, Russ considered as he looked at Rich now, easy-going with his hands in his pockets. Still, that medallion was around his neck.

"When you put it that way, Rich . . . well, guess you're right about that. We all fall down some time or another."

Rich acknowledged with a wink. "Well, come in, come in now. Hope you can stay like usual. I just put on another pot of coffee seeing that it was about time for you to stop by. In fact, you're early!"

Russ was already taking off his overshoes. "You bet I'm early, Rich. I'd never have guessed it, but the books all balanced this morning. That's a celebration right there!" He slapped the boots together not intending for so much snow to shake off on the floor. "Oops."

Rich laughed as he turned to go to the kitchen. "Glad to see you in a good mood, Russel. Take off your jacket and cap and let's see what goodies you brought this morning."

The scene was familiar at the kitchen table as the two drank their coffee and ate their cinnamon rolls, as if today was just any of the other days in the past three months after Rich's independence had become an issue. The morning ritual suited Russ—not more than an hour but just enough of a visit to catch up on news and chew the fat over a roll and cup of coffee, and to check in on a sick friend. Mostly, he preferred not even to think about the visits in that way, that Rich might never get any better but only worse. "After all, doctors sometimes are wrong," he'd say. But the reality of last night cloaked over Russ like that winter storm. Now, sitting face to face again with Rich, he felt a dull ache of something lost. Last night's episode was real—an alarm sounding in the dark, his buddy flat-out on a floor, emergency crews waiting—all warning signs. His able buddy was not so able anymore. Russ was troubled.

"Say, Rich . . ." he began after easing into the topic with a light-hearted exchange on slips and falls and older people living alone, the kind of light-hearted exchange about the travails of aging that includes an "Ole and Lena" joke or two. ". . . enough about the funny stuff. Now what exactly *does* your doctor say about travel—you know, like this cruise we're talking about? What about that?" He tapped his thumb on the coffee cup.

The grin on Rich's face faded, replaced with a tightening jaw. Shaking his head, he looked off to the kitchen window framed in ice crystals, "Oh, Russel," he finally said. "You know how much I'd like to go on that cruise . . ." The pause was longer than comfortable for an obvious answer so he stirred his coffee again, then took a loud sip. He turned back to face Russ. "But the fact is: It's just not going to work for me to go! I've got all these darned medicines to take." He turned to point at the row of pill bottles lining his countertop like a spice rack. "Then there are the doctor appointments and always tests, and more tests, at the hospital." Seeing the dark prediction casting a gloom over his friend's face, he paused. Like one trained in the art of engaging others, he formed a wry smile. Mimicking a doctor peering over his glasses, he said in a very low-pitch, "Let's see, Mr. Frederiksen, you will be seeing me at least once a week from now until *eternity*." Back in his regular voice, he responded to the invisible doctor, "Oh, yes, you know how much I enjoy my doctor visits and *all* the tests and medicines. I just can't wait for my next appointment!"

Still the face across the table was sullen, not to be budged. Rich readjusted his glasses, "Okay, okay, Russel, so it's not exactly funny. Really, the fact of the matter is I don't have the energy anymore. For heaven's sake, just getting up every day is a big deal. And my kids, well, they'd have a fit worrying." He threw out his hands with a shrug.

Russ resumed stirring his coffee, still not ready to comment, sensing the dark alley where this was going.

"Why do you think I've got this danged medallion around my neck, huh?" The statement had a bite which seemed to have been hiding just under the skin until now. He grabbed the alarm jewelry piece and held it out in front of Russ. "This is as *good* as it gets for someone in my shape. At least I can be in my own house! Just think of it that way, Russel." He leaned back, took a couple of deep, long breaths, and patted the medallion against his chest. "Yes, sir, I can be in my own house."

Russ adjusted his chair back a step. Never before had Rich complained to him or raised his voice even the slightest, and after the ordeal last night, Russ didn't think he needed to be reminded about the jewelry's purpose. He folded his arms across his chest and slunk a bit in his chair.

Neither said a word as the clock in the next room ticked on, amplified, it seemed. Russ started tapping his foot in double-time with the clock. Eventually, Rich's stare across the room transformed into a sly and gentle smile again. "Besides, think of all the stories you can tell me, huh? Stories about you and the guys. Think of *that*, Russel." He chuckled softly with his eyes closed. "Just picture it: You and Elmer and Hubert and Wilbur . . . you know, Russel, that's funny already."

Russ stopped tapping and eyed Rich as if what he had said bordered on the ridiculous. Yet, Russ knew full-well his angle. "Stories, hell!" he snapped. "And what's this you say about me and the guys? For Pete's sake, Rich, do you know what you're saying? I'm practically their social planner now, driving them everywhere. They're just sitting in their houses until I call and say to them, 'Let's go eat somewhere, boys.' And then they're all for it—*sure*, all they need to know is what time I'm coming by to pick them up. And do you think they'd ever fill up the tank? Hell, no. Well, that is, except for a couple bucks here and there—but it's almost never." Russ sat up straight in his chair with his fists on his hips, his eyes bouncing like pin balls. Rich knew to let him finish.

"Take Elmer, for instance. Well, I have to say, he's a good old boy, that's for sure. He'll join in on just about anything—but, Rich, do you know he's almost *ninety-three* now? That's getting right up there, wouldn't you say? *Ninety-three* . . . Holy Moses, that's when my dad died! And here we are, talking about old Elmer taking a big trip like this. For cripes sakes, I'd be worrying about him getting around at the airport, on the boat, you know, hell-knows-where!" Russ paused in exasperation but Rich was only nodding in agreement with a patient smile.

"Then there's Hubert—*sure* he'll go along. Hell, he and his wife traveled the world, for gosh sake—more than any of the rest of us, that's for sure. But now that his wife's gone and he's on his own, he just doesn't say much—lets everyone else do the talking. Why if it wasn't for our bunch, he'd still be eating Meals on Wheels and staying put on his butt in his living room. Besides, he looks owlier than hell most of the time with that turned-down-mouth of his—it makes people nervous." Russ tapped his thumb on the table as he thought more about the group's misgivings and any possible reason at all why group travel might not be in their best interest. Rich continued to nod and smile.

"And Wilbur, the teetotaler, the *good* Methodist . . . shoot, I want to enjoy a drink if I want one, damn it!" Russ fidgeted with his coffee cup, a little embarrassed to be nit-picking. "Plus . . . well . . . his face gets so red—like that time at the State Fair—looked like he was ready to pop right there at the John Deere display!" Russ looked up from his cup for any sign from Rich. "What if he just keeled over? What about that?" Russ reared up from the table and began to pace the kitchen. "This has turned into *me* driving everyone around and planning their social events! You know as well I do that we've *never* been invited to their houses, not once . . . well, except for Elmer and his boys. Just once I'd like one of them to take charge!" Russ stopped pacing and raised his arms out in desperation. "Richard, I need your advice!"

Rich, still with that patient smile, straightened up and with his hand on Russ's chair motioned for him. "Russel, Russel, sit back down and just let me talk now. You'll be fine, just fine." Russ with his arms folded now didn't budge. "Russel, you might not have everything in common with those guys but, gosh darn, they're our bunch—think about it—we've been almost like a family these last six years. Sure, they can't cook a meal, and maybe their driving isn't so good anymore, and maybe they're a little forgetful, and maybe they hold on to their money too tight, but Russel—we're *all* getting up there in age! The fact is: We need to stick together. What else do we have?" Russel, I know you pretty well . . . and Russel, I know it's *not* your favorite thing to eat by yourself. Isn't that so, huh?" Russ didn't answer except for a shift of his eyes. "And I know that deep down, Russel, you get a kick out of hauling those old guys around—it keeps you on your toes, keeps you young." Rich paused with a quiet sigh as Russ settled back in his chair. "Besides, Russel, that cruise ship is a *big* boat—a really, really *big* boat—and you can do what you want to most of the time, get away by yourself. Hey, maybe you'll find some lonely widows on that boat, you never know, Russel." The roguish smile erased years off Rich's face.

As Russ was about to respond, Rich raised his finger for a final point. "This much I know: You *must* go, and you *must* have a good time. Just imagine—a week in the tropics, away from this winter weather. I know for certain, Russel, that you'd kick yourself later if you passed up this opportunity. And that's what this is—an opportunity. For heaven's sake, that's what you always say: 'Get out there and do things!' Admit it, Russel, that's what you always say: '*Do* things!' Don't disappoint me, Russel!" Whipped up now like an evangelist, Rich couldn't help but raise his arms in his feverish pitch and look upward as if pleading to someone above. He paused in that position, his eyes diverting from the kitchen ceiling to Russ, looking for a cue. He could see he hit a nerve.

Somewhat taken aback being reminded of his own philosophy, Russ nodded in agreement with a trance-like gaze. "Yeah, Richard, I've got to say that you're right—that *is* what I've said . . . ah huh . . . *do* things . . ."

Rich rested his elbows back on the table and reached for his coffee cup. "Besides, I have a feeling that after you get back we'll have a lot of time to catch up, and who knows, I might be ready to kick up my heels again." He leaned back and clicked his soft slippers together under the table, and sat up straight with an over-energetic grin. "So that's it then—you and the guys talk to that travel agent again this week to get this set up. I'll put in my two cents with the planning. Right here from my house, I'll help with the planning." He swallowed the last of his coffee and set the empty mug back on the table with a firm thud.

Russ shifted his eyes back to Rich. "Are you done?"

"Yup."

Russ straightened up a bit in his chair. "All I can say is: I'll think about it. I have to admit, well, you are absolutely right about some things." Russ tapped his fingers on the edge of the table in a slow, steady beat. "I know that your oldest boy out there on the farm is the other one listed by that medical place to call if you need some help, right? That is, if, for instance, I wasn't around to answer the phone." He looked over his glasses at Rich for a firm answer.

Rich nodded with a confident smile.

The finger cadence slowed even more. "And it would be just *one* week . . ." Russ got up from the table and walked to the calendar on the kitchen wall. He turned the pages to March. "Hmm . . ." He flipped the pages back and sat down again at the table and drank the last of his coffee. "Well, let's not talk about it anymore today." The statement was crisp like a judge closing a case. He glanced toward the window with the ice crystals catching the morning sun now. "Say, Rich, did you hear the weather report that we got nine inches last night? And now just look at that bright, blue sky. Isn't it something?"

Rich glanced at the window too, but was more interested that Russ had started a soft whistle. "You don't say. Nine?"

"You bet. Nine, with plenty of drifts. And believe me, I should know . . ." He shot a teasing glance at Rich who nodded back and smiled. "And I hear another front is coming in next week." Russ leaned back and started a slow tap of his foot. "Yeah, that was one heck of a night, one heck of a night for sure . . ."

Russ continued to whistle under his breath, and the two seemed content with their own thoughts as the clock chimed the hour.

CHAPTER 2
UNTIL DEATH

So much for "the golden years." Anyone with that idea has another think coming, that's for damned sure. Russ brooded. Six years before the notion as exotic as a cruise ever crossed his mind, he was barely just a passing acquaintance with the guys who might in fact be bunking with him for a week in the Caribbean. That was when he found himself strangely alone and without much to say, which says a lot about the circumstances for the storyteller in town.

He fiddled with the keys in his pocket as he paced around the open trunk of his car, waiting for his daughters, thinking about "the golden years." "What the hell's taking them so long," he finally muttered out loud as he kicked a piece of gravel across the asphalt, then sheepishly looked around to see if anyone was near enough to hear him say the word "hell" out there in the parking lot of St. John's Lutheran Church. Only half a dozen cars remained at the church property. The Bittners who were just backing up from their parking space across the lot smiled with tight lips and nodded as they passed by him, their windows rolled up tight. Russ nodded back but kept his hands in his pockets.

"Dad! There you are! You must have skipped out when we were busy talking to the ladies in the kitchen. We were figuring out where all the food was going to go." A daughter, who in fact had just lost her spouse, was hurrying to the car with a floral arrangement in each hand, tiptoeing as she tried to run in her high heels, and behind her he could see two other daughters and their husbands, all carrying baskets and containers. Tagging behind them were the ten grandkids, the oldest, who was in college, now carrying the youngest, a toddler, on his shoulders with the others hanging together as a group, relieved to be free of the stagnant air in the church basement and one step apart somehow from the adult world of grief. Russ immediately welled up with pride seeing his good-looking family coming across the parking lot, and for a split second he could see himself again as a young boy, like one of those grandsons, fresh and energetic, oblivious to life's serious side. He loosened his tie.

"Yeah, well the trunk can hold most of that stuff, and we have the other two cars too. Let's load it all up and head for the house. We can figure out what goes where once we get there. I was beginning to wonder what the heck was taking you so long." He wiped his forehead with a brusque swipe of his sleeve and began loading the trunk. "Gol darn, it's starting to get hot out here!"

The funeral service that morning, he'd be the first to point out, was as nice as any he'd attended in his seventy-six years. He was satisfied that a good turnout of relatives and towns-people filled most of the pews, including half a dozen from the VFW Ladies Auxiliary who were impressive with their matching blue blazers and white pants and the formal way they paraded into the sanctuary to the roped-off pew. He liked that the minister wasn't long-winded, which old Reverend Woodstrom tended to be more often than not. He also took notice that even on this hot August day, the old Lutheran church, stuffy with its ornate figurines and dark heavy wood, was comfortable with a little breeze through the side windows—those beautiful tall stained-glass windows so rich in detailed color and symbols, yet practical for a guy like himself to appreciate, with a lower hinged section that opened to the outdoors. Just enough flower memorials, and a nice variety at that, decorated the steps to the altar. People noticed these kinds of things about funerals Russ was told, and also, who cried and who didn't. So he made special note of these things during the service, checking off a mental list similar to what Lorraine might do. Since this was really about Lorraine, he felt okay that he didn't pay particular attention to Pastor Woodstrom. Instead, his mind wandered as he gazed at the spray of forty-eight long-stemmed red roses he personally ordered—forty-eight for the years he and Lorraine were married. That had been his standard anniversary gift, adding a rose each year. The two years he missed, that was '44 and '45 when he was off fighting in Europe, he made up that first week he was back home. Always assuming they would reach fifty years, and now as he sat on that hard pew, counting and re-counting the forty-eight roses, he felt short-changed. The satin ribbon read "Loving Wife."

The interment service was on a hot, windy hill at the city cemetery just a couple miles out of town, surrounded by fields of corn and soybeans. Back in the fifties, the stately row of elm trees died off from Dutch elm disease so now the hill was barren except for the tall headstones and a couple of small evergreens. Still, it was a good, familiar place that Lorraine would like, and it suited her, raised a quiet, plain, farm girl.

Afterward, St. John's Ladies Aid served lunch back in the church basement. Over the years, Lorraine did her share of funeral lunches so now, Russ reconciled, she was on the receiving end. With summer weather too warm and humid for the usual Lutheran fare of hot-dishes, instead today the ladies served cold ham sandwiches and several noodle salads, along with the usual Jell-O molds, yellow cake, and of course, coffee. Russ choked down part of a ham sandwich with his cup of coffee, then pushed his plate away.

The ordeal had him worn out. The house had been crowded for two days now with the three daughters and their families back home and no one getting much sleep. "The final arrangements,' as the funeral director referred to this process, seemed anything but "final," as the details dragged on, involving always more phone calls, more decisions. And on this day of the funeral, wearing his suit and tie, which he last wore at his daughter's wedding two years ago, he felt cramped and itchy. Without Lorraine to banter about what he should or shouldn't wear, he argued with himself that morning to rationalize his distraction from the sadness that gnawed. Feeling more like a stranger watching from the sidelines than a loving husband of forty-eight years, he simply took it in.

Sitting, waiting, standing around—anyone in town could vouch that those weren't his strong suits but that's what was dealt out these past few days. The conversations were as rigid as the church pews. Even those folks that he figured should know better—friends through the years—even they fumbled for the right words with their faces tight and nervous, their eyes shifting to another part of the room or at the floor. Mad as hell for having actually to help them with their words, he wanted it out with them. "Come on now," he wanted to say, "speak up! Life is about death too, it's part of the deal! Why should anyone be awkward about it? When your time is up, that's it, so you'd better make the best of your time!"

He'd seen his share of dying in the war, and that had cast a rational layer to his view on any of his personal losses since. Hell, he could talk plenty about personal losses, even to include a daughter. Now Lorraine. But this wasn't the time to lecture on anything, let alone dying, he reminded himself. Instead, he was that stranger in the uncomfortable clothes looking in from the sidelines, catching bits of conversation about the weather, the crops, and the whereabouts of grown children.

By early evening, the two daughters who lived some hours away drove off for home, but the youngest daughter from her farm nearby agreed with her sisters to stay the night, one night anyway. Too numb to argue, Russ consented. So instead of a visit to the river valley where a guy like Russ could rely on finding relief and solace, he took a couple of aspirin for his headache, and the two of them settled in front of the television for the night, not really watching but not really talking either.

She leafed through the sympathy cards and memorials as the television droned, but soon she nodded off in her chair. How odd, he thought, to see a daughter there and not Lorraine.

Russ didn't sleep that night. The headache was replaced by a dull ache throughout his body as if trapped in a too-small space and a restlessness that made him toss and turn, as his mind relived scenes from the last few days—the doctor peering over his little glasses with his grim report, Lorraine ghostly-pale in that hospital bed hooked up to tubes and monitors, the sudden call in the middle of the night, the cremation director in his dark suit describing urns. As he drifted in and out of sleep, the images blurred and jumbled with bizarre twists, as dreams do, so that he woke in a sweat with heart racing, lay there in the darkness remembering, and then drifted off again to yet more frightening scenes.

Finally with daybreak now visible through the shaded window, Russ glanced at the clock to confirm it, then relaxed back on his pillow. Staring at the ceiling, hands folded on his chest, he pondered the realities of his new life: Right off the bat, it was a house guest that had his attention—he needed to send her home. Russ felt a surge of energy, realizing his task at hand, like a new-found purpose for this vacant day. Well-meaning, that's what she was, and he was damn proud of her, but no way in hell was it a good situation for him to be dependent upon anyone for the sake of anything—conversation, meals, or what have you. He remembered old Jake Johnson down the block whose kids hung around so much after his wife died that old Jake never really left the house again. He just waited for his kids to show up. Then pretty soon the kids didn't come around that often and before long he was carted off to a nursing home—word in the pool hall was he even needed someone to bath him and hand-feed him, just like a baby. Like a death sentence, that's what it was. No, sir, what a guy needs is to buckle down and figure it out, no matter what the situation—get back to a routine, let the Good Lord show you the way, just like He always does. This is how it should be. Russ closed his eyes briefly in sort of an "amen" and then rolled out of bed to his shoes parked there on the floor.

He busied himself in the kitchen rattling dishes intentionally to wake up his daughter sleeping in the room just above. He heated water for his instant coffee, sliced a grapefruit, and dropped a couple pieces of bread in the toaster. While he waited, and as a matter of ritual, he checked the outdoor thermometer on the wall in the next room—"Hmm, seventy degrees already and still so early in the morning . . ." He tapped the barometer—it was steady. "Yup, another hot one again." The ease of rituals. Back in the kitchen, he switched on the kitchen radio to WCCO to get the full weather report and then reached for the jelly jar in the refrigerator.

His daughter appeared in the kitchen door with a big yawn and stretch, but dressed for the day and eager to help with breakfast, make conversation, and otherwise soften the reality in even a small way. "'Morning, Dad. How'd you sleep?"

Russ closed the refrigerator and set the jelly on the table. He looked at her with no particular warmth and as if surprised that she would be awake at this hour. "Oh, you're up. Yeah, good morning." Glad for something to do, he grabbed the whistling teapot from the stove and poured into the two mugs. "Sleep, you say? Hell, I just lay there all night—guess it was too damned hot. Couldn't wait for morning." His voice was still raspy from the night. He grabbed silverware and plates for the two of them, keeping his head low to the task and muttering but still intentionally loud enough so his daughter would be sure to hear, ". . . but I told myself, so what! I need to get down to the station early anyhow since I've missed so many hours of work this week." He paused just a second to emphasize what he had just stated. His eyes shifted towards her. "You, on the other hand, can get back home to tend to your family. And there's your job too—don't forget that. I got to thinking through all that last night. Your boss is going to wonder . . ."

"No, no, Dad. Slow down a minute . . . it's fine. I don't have to go in today—you know, with the funeral and everything. I'll just hang around and help with things here. Later I'll check in with what's going on at home. And I'll call my boss again today, I promise.

Russ buttered the toast. He wasn't in the mood to be coaxed. "Grapefruit isn't very good this time of year, but Mom and I bought some anyway—Safeway in New Ulm had a good price. Mom saw the ad and thought we should get at least a few." He paused a second, mid-buttering, realizing how particularly easy it was to talk about Lorraine—not dead, not laying out there in the city cemetery plot—but shopping for grapefruit. That sort of topic might otherwise be the biggest issue of the day. Comforting, that's how it was, just the topic of grapefruit.

The daughter busied herself setting the table, waiting for her dad to finish, not noticing the far-away look in his eyes.

He cleared his throat. "Ah . . . anyway, you can't beat Texas grapefruit whether they're in season or not." He continued with the toast, slathering on more butter than usual. His movements were quick and exact as he ran a knife through the toast. "Yeah, like I said, you can head on home as soon as we're done here, and I'll get down to the books at the station. Heaven knows, those young kids clerking there now always seem to mess up the receipts, so I'll have my hands full getting that straightened out."

"I don't think anyone is expecting you back at the station today, Dad. For goodness sake, the funeral was just yesterday—you can just take it easy, do something else. Thought maybe you and I could go on a little drive somewhere . . . I can fix some dinner later on . . . Rich and the kids will probably drive over to visit tonight . . . whatever you want to do . . . you can . . ."

Russ snapped the plate of toast on the table. His face couldn't hide the irritation welling up inside. "Wait just a minute, hold on now. That might be okay for some—but not for me!" Still with the butter knife in his hand and pointing to himself like an exhibit at trial, he barked again, "Not for me!" Adrenaline pumped like a kind of super fuel.

That kind of bark had never ever been directed to her before, but his daughter knew the look well—those eyes that meant business, a look that meant no one would be changing his mind anytime soon. He set the knife down and put two more slices of bread in the toaster. Attempting to sound reasonable, he lowered his voice. "Seems to me a guy needs to get back to doing his regular routine, you know, responsibilities. You ask me what I want to do—well, I'm saying, that's what I want to do—my regular routine. How else is a guy going to stand on his own two feet? Just like you have your responsibilities too . . . your family, your job . . . but it sure the hell isn't taking care of me!" Those last words seemed to tumble out from someone less reasonable.

She slunk back, folding her arms tight across her chest. With her eyes open wide and unblinking to hold back the tears welling up, she mustered one last attempt. "Ah, I understand what you're saying, Dad, but . . ."

"Take me for example: I've got a job to go to, people depending on me, and I've got lots to keep me busy besides that. You sure as heck don't want to be sitting around here waiting for me to go on a drive somewhere, or wasting your time getting a meal together for me. *I* can cook—heck, it will do me good to figure it out. Sure, it's a hell of a shame to lose Mom like that, so sudden. There's no good reason for it, none. I just have a bad feeling about those damned doctors and what they didn't tell us . . ." His jaw clenched. ". . . but that's it, there's no turning back the pages—we just go on from here." Now it was his eyes welling up so he grabbed his handkerchief from his pocket. "Damn it!" He blew his nose hard, then turned up the volume on the radio. "Now let's sit down and eat our breakfast!"

"Okay, okay, Dad." She reached across the table and patted his shoulder. His shoulder stiffened. He reached for the cream.

They settled in on eating their grapefruit and toast with WCCO morning news blaring from the kitchen counter, both of them thankful for the news reports to fill the clumsy silence. Between bites, Russ fidgeted with his whirring hearing aid, which other times would have annoyed him but today was another helpful avoidance tactic. Between bites, Deb sniffed to control her drippy nose. This would be the only discussion from then on with any of the daughters considering Russ' ability to manage on his own.

"Sure was nice to see a good crowd show up yesterday . . . yes, siree . . ." He swallowed the last of his coffee, then leaned back in his chair and finally looked across the table at the daughter, his youngest, who he noticed today looked far too worried and sad for her twenty-nine years. His face softened. "Oh, don't forget to take a couple of those plants along with you when you go—would look real nice in your new house. And those cards with money in them, you said that you girls got that all written down someplace . . . so let's look at those the next time you're here, you know, write those thank yous, just like you mentioned. I'll take care of the deposit on Monday."

The daughter took her time loading the car, considering her dad might have a change of heart. But like a prod, he tagged at her heels. "Remember, Dad, you have all those leftovers in the frig—the cold cuts, some Jell-O, noodle salad, also hotdish from the neighbors . . ."

"Right, right . . . I'll take a look . . . now is that it? You have everything?"

"Ah, huh, that's it." She closed the trunk and turned to him. "Now, you know, we're not that far away. If you need anything . . . anything . . . just give us a call. And besides that, we'll be over soon, probably tomorrow, but I'll call first. Sounds like you might be, oh, maybe a little hard to catch . . ." She gave him a "got you" look.

He smiled. "Yeah, just give me a call."

"Okay, well, I'll be seeing you soon then . . ." She patted his shoulder with a polite hug but he grabbed her in close just for a second or two.

"Thank you now for all you girls did. Everything turned out real nice."

She nodded and wiped away the tears that were spilling down her face. Not able to say the sad thoughts consuming her, she simply smiled and then got in the car and turned the ignition. "Bye, see you soon, Dad."

As she straightened the car out on the street, she looked back at him and waved. Her dad, small and wiry, now from this distance and framed by her childhood home looked particularly thin and old as he stood there alone with shoulders a little slumped. She hesitated . . . then slowly drove off.

He watched her round the corner until she was out of sight, as parents do, but this time it was more like he was the one driving off to a new kind of independence. *Strange, the turns that life takes*, he thought. A mourning dove cooed from the neighbor's old shed across the street and then flew to the telephone wire overhead where Russ couldn't help but notice. He admired it, with its iridescent feathers glistening in the sun. "Well, Lorraine," he said quietly as he watched the bird preening its feathers, "we raised some good girls, all right," and then he walked back to get into his car to head to the station.

Russ, Wilbur, Elmer, and Hubert at Vernon Park with bicyclists.

CHAPTER 3
BALANCE SHEETS

The two tellers at Morgan State Bank were visiting over the divider at their stations waiting for the morning business when Russ walk in. They chimed, "'Morning, Russ!" like cheerleaders. This was the usual reception for Russ because they especially liked him, always friendly and outgoing and most often with a story or two. And like clock-work, he arrived at the bank every weekday morning with his 9:30 deposit for the Texaco Oil station. Some townspeople would say right up front that Russ was the best deal that Texaco owner Dwight ever made, employing someone with Russ's aptitude and quickness with numbers, integrity, and loyalty to boot—all for minimum wage. "Hey, it's a great job for a retired old guy like Russ," Dwight always defended. "Besides, I'm letting him do it his way, by hand, and not making him learn the computer like most businesses now." Russ never did let talk of this nature bother him—he figured the job suited him just fine.

On some days Russ might have a deposit for another account too—the Morgan Beneficial Society—that's if a member had recently "kicked off," as he put it. For each death, Russ collected the fees, four dollars per person, for a lump-sum death benefit of not quite

$1,000, which was not quite enough to cover even the most basic burial costs, but a sound and simple plan nevertheless for the small farming community. Russ had stepped into this managing role of the self-funded insurance plan some twenty years ago when old Judge Fisher became too blind and frail to continue the duties any longer. Those duties included hand-writing a couple hundred post-cards after a death to notify the members that their payments were due, collecting the payments, which many times were dropped off in person, and finally issuing the benefit check to the bereaved family. Russ took to the role naturally with his ledger books, Papermate pen, and adding machine at his desk in the basement where he meticulously organized everything of importance. Important things for Russ happened to include not only these fiduciary duties but his duck stamp collection from the past fifty years.

And on some days, Russ might have a deposit in another capacity—as administrator of an estate. The word in Morgan was that you couldn't beat the likes of Russ Albrecht when it came down to numbers and honesty, so folks in the area sought him out for such details in handling their financial matters at life's end. He could recite all of the regulations of the *Minnesota Estate Administration Manual*, and frequently would do so in explaining his calculations to the deceased's family when perhaps they revealed a greedy intention. He knew, too, a bit about resolving family conflicts over, say, how the farmland should be divided. And he always had a story or two and a shot of brandy if someone were to stop by his house late-morning to talk through the estate details. Brandy in the morning was an elixir that he learned from old Oscar Hanson. That's back when Russ first gardened a plot of old Oscar's land at the east edge of town. Oscar always had a quart of Mr. Boston in the shed when Russ stopped for a break from weeding. But one shot was it and only in the morning, then back to business. Russ liked that sort of rapport, and so it was in Russ' basement, tending to financial matters.

With this sort of high esteem from the community, it was only natural that Russ also earned the tellers' respect, a respect mixed with a bit of nervousness, like the effect of an auditor's visit.

"Good morning!" He addressed both of them with a smile, which was forced today and with a tired cast to his eyes. "I've got a sizeable deposit this morning after missing work a couple of days in a row." He reached in the leather bank pouch and brought out a stack of checks and a stack of bills, and then he emptied the coins at the counter with great flourish in front of Linda to dramatize the size of the deposit. "There. That'll take you a minute or two to count all that up!" His fingers began to drum on the counter.

"Wow, this definitely is more than a day's worth!" Linda stopped a quarter from rolling off the counter and plopped it back on the stack of change with a nervous giggle. "There!" Short on small talk today, the giggle worked as filler, but still she was embarrassed by it. Seeing her favorite customer now with this heavy face and a slump to his shoulders, not his usual wiry self, she wished she could just give him a hug. She knew very well another side to this man particularly impatient today, clocking her work. Stories had circulated in the bank about Russ's special care for a bank officer with Lou Gehrig's disease a couple years back—a vet from World War II like Russ. Right up until the end, it was told, Russ made daily visits and saw to it that this vet's wife had the support she needed.

Russ's fingers were still drumming, his eyes fixed on the stack of money.

"So sorry to hear about Lorraine!" she blurted, looking at him straight-on, but with her hands still busy removing the binder off the stack of bills. Her eyes welled up, now having said it. She opened her eyes wide to keep from blinking and spilling the tears. Seeing Russ wince, she ducked back to the deposit slip and began to count the cash, stopping only to reach under the counter to grab a tissue for her eyes.

Carol, the other teller, listening from the next window, was nodding in agreement as she dabbed both index fingers under her eyes to stop her mascara from running further. She leaned her head just out of the window. "Yes, Russ, if there's anything we can do, anything . . ." Her voice faded when her lip began to quiver. Tight-lipped, she chose just to nod again in agreement at the sadness of it all.

Women crying for whatever reason gave Russ a knot in his stomach like a bad meal, and having raised four daughters, he knew it well. Now hoping to fend off yet more emotions, he looked away too, conveniently at the clock just behind them on the wall. Then he glanced at his watch, the way one might to double-check the time. Linda was back to an all-business mode with the deposit, but still sniffing. He stopped drumming and put his hands in his pocket, then began jiggling his keys.

"Yeah, married forty-eight years. . . . Wanted to get to fifty and have a special golden celebration like my folks, the big cake and party . . . but didn't quite make it. Nowadays though with all the divorces going on, forty-eight is pretty darned good, don't you think?" Looking at the practical side, he figured these young women could relate to the likelihood of divorce cutting a marriage short more than they could relate to death. Divorce had been on his mind anyway because the middle daughter had divorced her wayward Texan husband and just last year had remarried, this time to a heck of a nice guy, Russ and Lorraine agreed. Lorraine had enjoyed herself so much at that wedding reception, getting that daughter a husband again and a father for those two kids. But it was just a few months later that Lorraine showed signs of the cancer returning. "Yeah, cancer and divorce can sure cut a guy's chances on making it to fifty years. Ah, huh . . . forty-eight, that's where we ended up . . ."

The girls managed weak smiles, nodding in agreement. Linda choked, "Oh, Russ, I know that you and Lorraine had a good life together, and forty-eight years is something to be treasured." She wiped her eyes again and resumed keying the numbers.

Russ cleared his throat. "Oh, before I forget, tell your boss that the bunch of flowers from the bank was real nice—those big yellow ones. I think those were Lorraine's favorites. Mums, I think . . . yeah, mums. Real pretty. Those I took home with me. Most of the others went out to Gil-Mor Manor for the residents there, one stayed at the church, and then some, of course, my daughters took." He looked at his watch again and then tapped his fingers on his sleeves as he whistled a non-descript tune under his breath.

36

"You bet, Russ, I'll be sure to tell him. Yes, let's see, I'll hurry along with this and be done in a minute." Her fingers were flying now. She printed out the receipt and handed it to him with a loving smile and put her other hand over his in such a caring manner Russ could only swallow hard and wait for the tightness in his throat to ease. "You have a good day now, and we'll look forward to seeing you tomorrow. And, you know, Russ," she pretended to look stern and motherly, "we haven't heard one of your fishing stories in a long, long while—you'd better get right down to the river and try your luck!" She tapped his hand.

Startled, but relieved with the lighter mood, Russ perked up. "Oh, fishing . . . yeah, well . . ." He managed a chuckle and then nodded thank you for her kind gesture as he slipped his hand back so he could put the receipt in the bank pouch. "You're right about that, Linda. I haven't been fishing in a long time . . . so much going on, you know, with doctor appointments and all that." Sensing an immediate heat to his face just at the word "doctor," he caught himself from going on further about the trials of a terminal illness, a topic not much suited for these young women. "Yeah, too much going on for me to be fishing . . . but then the river has been too high, and walleye fishing never gets good until about September anyway." He zipped up the pouch neatly and turned to go with a polite grin. "I'll sure let you gals know though—about the fishing, that is. Sure will. Well, guess I'm done here. I'll see you same time tomorrow." He tipped his cap goodbye.

"See you, Russ," they chimed again. Both girls, still sniffing, waved goodbye as Russ walked away, and then they turned to each other, nodding their sentiments across the divider of the teller booths.

Russ stopped at the door to hold it open for a young couple coming into the bank. He couldn't help but notice the new faces, fresh and eager—and so different from the glum world where he now found himself. The couple seemed to carry along with them a breath of fresh air, which got his attention like pure oxygen. Sure, that's it, he remembered now—the young man he recognized from a picture last month in the paper—one of the new teachers at the high school, coming from the Twin Cities. He liked that kind of news. A small farming town like Morgan could use a boost with more of these young families. "'Morning!" he greeted them with the enthusiasm of a welcome committee.

Startled by such an exuberant greeting so early in the day by this older man and complete stranger, the couple hesitated, almost stumbling into each other. As Russ stepped by them and on out the door with a friendly wave, they returned the smile and waved back. "Ah . . . yes . . . good morning to you, sir, and thank you! Have a good day!" the young man spoke up after Russ before the door closed.

"Nice gentleman!" he said as he and his wife approached the tellers, each still with a tissue in hand. "Must be how small towns treat their new teachers!" His face brimmed with pleasure, not even noticing the tellers' watery eyes.

"Yes, a very, very, nice gentleman," Linda said, setting her tissue aside. Then snapping to attention with the business at hand, she smiled at the eager, fresh faces. "So, you are new in town. Welcome to Morgan! What can we do for you today?

Russ paused a minute on the bank steps, drinking in the pleasant thought of that young couple making a home in Morgan. A darned good place to raise a family, he mulled. He looked across Vernon Avenue towards the pool hall, the next stop in his normal routine—a stop for coffee and maybe to chew the fat or play a hand of Schnozel with the farmers in town for their morning break. He could even tell them about bumping into the new teacher. Across the street he saw old Emil Ludwig park his new Ford Ranger in front of the pool hall, and he saw Gordy the barber leaving his shop heading down the sidewalk in that direction. "Naw, not today, Russ" he reprimanded himself under his breath, his conscience firm with instructions on what was and what wasn't the proper thing to do just one day after a funeral. Lorraine would see it that way too. He turned to walk to his car. "I'll just make my usual stop at the post office, that's what I'll do."

The mail box was stuffed, so Russ had to cradle all the pieces in his arms to get the stack into his car—the usual utility bills, Morgan's weekly newspaper, *The Messenger*, some ads, mostly from neighboring towns, a thick envelope from the University of Minnesota Hospital, several envelopes addressed to Morgan Beneficial Society care of Russel Albrecht, and probably a dozen cards addressed either "Family of Lorraine Albrecht" or "Russel Albrecht & Girls." He didn't relish looking at more of those cards, but at the same time was curious enough when he got back in his car to flick through the envelopes to read the return addresses. One caught his eye—from the Ladies Auxiliary Post 49, likely a memorial. Lorraine, of course, had been a member all those years since the war, marched in the parades, put wreaths at the cemetery each Memorial Day. Funny how life works, he thought mesmerized by the embossed script of the return address with a little U.S. flag in the corner, "Here I am—made it through the whole damned war, shot twice and pneumonia besides, and Lorraine too, she suffered plenty back then, just getting it through those years alone with two small kids—then here down the line, when things should be easier, she ends up with cancer."

Someone was tapping on his door. Startled, Russ turned to look. It was Roy Hanson stooped over with his face about an inch from the window. Russ rolled it down, "Well, hi there, Roy. Ah, you kind of surprised me! How are you doing?" Russ shoved the stack of mail to the side and then looked up at the eager face.

"Hello, Russel. Oh, I'm fine, fine. I wanted to catch you just to say . . . .well, I just wanted to give you . . . you know . . . . my condolences. I'm not much one for funerals—it was yesterday, was it?"

"Sure was, Roy. Yeah, had a houseful for a few days."

Roy shuffled and looked down at his feet, "Yeah, I heard that you were having a tough time taking care of your wife, getting her to the doctors real fast and all . . . I, ah . . . well, the guys at the pool hall were talking about it, you know. I just wanted to let you know . . ."

"I sure do appreciate that, Roy. Thank you very much." Russ had learned that speaking to Roy in a deliberate manner smoothed out the communication. Roy had suffered a stroke probably a year ago now and had appointed Russ with power of attorney. His words often slurred, but his mind was pretty sharp, just not sharp enough to trust himself with financial matters any more. That's where Russ came in.

Roy was a bachelor who had farmed his whole life, but now, with no family left and physically limited with the stroke, he had to give up farming. He finally moved into town in the spring, there on the east side next to the highway, into what could easily be mistaken for a shed, no bigger really than a couple of rooms. But in this tiny house and with Russ' help, Roy was able to manage on his own.

"You know, Roy, I'll be up to your house here . . . oh, later in the week . . . and we'll go over all your bills. It's just about the end of the month so we'll get your things all cleared up again for you. How does that sound?"

"Now, Russel, I don't want you to worry about my stuff right now. You see, my things can wait. I'm doing okay. Don't you worry about me—just wanted to tell you, you know, about not getting to the funeral." He straightened up and steadied himself with his hand on the door. "So, I'll let you go now . . . ah, I know that you're always so busy . . . always got things to do." He turned to leave.

Russ had always respected Roy's silent toughness. At this moment, old Roy seemed like a refreshing drink. "Say, I'll tell you what, Roy," Russ spoke up, "on second thought, here's a better idea: I'll stop by *tomorrow*, in fact! About this time after I pick up my mail. Okay?"

Roy turned back and leaned down to the window again. "Tomorrow?" His face had brightened like an eager boy. "Well . . . ah . . . sure, Russel! That would be just fine. Tomorrow. Okay then, I'll let you go . . . I'll be seeing you . . . tomorrow!" He tapped Russ on the shoulder, adjusted his cap, and then headed to his car.

The stroke also had left Roy with a slight limp, but not so much that he needed a cane—he just walked slower than most, with an uneven step and a floppy foot. It was his spirit, that toughness in what life dishes out to you, that got Russ's attention. Roy always seemed to have a smile as wide as his face, and he'd drop what he was doing to take time to visit. "That's what people notice first off when they meet a person," Russ would instruct his young girls. "That's what really matters," he'd tell them.

Russ watched him walk to his car, gangly with that uneven step, some would say a bit broken—but not really, Russ knew.

CHAPTER 4
TENDER MERCIES

The mower started right up which prompted Russ to thank the good Lord for the second time that day. Eager to prove a point that good things can happen even in dark times, Russ was keeping count. The first little blessing that day was spotting a pair of wild turkeys crossing the road that morning as he drove along the river bottom near his ten acres of hard woods. A spotting like this was a good indication that the DNR guys were absolutely right with their prediction in the *Star Tribune* last summer that wild turkeys would be making a comeback in the valley, soothing news for a guy like Russ who centered himself with the checks and balances of nature.

Something now like his mower not starting up, for instance, needing several pulls on the cord, which happened more often than not, and causing that shortness of breath he was experiencing more and more these days, certainly wouldn't have turned Russ into a skeptic on life, but he would have been mad as hell. Mad that those damned cigarettes which Uncle Sam handed out in the war—those damned cigarettes which were included in every C-ration—now had done the damage and left his lungs something less than what the lungs of a seventy-six-year-old guy ought to be so that a simple task of starting a lawn mower could be a major hurdle. So the roar of the motor with the puff of exhaust was another bit of favor that Russ was happy to acknowledge. "Yes, siree," he coached himself, "he's still watching over me," and he briskly pushed the mower along the driveway up to the front sidewalk as he began to edge the yard.

Neighbor Al Tillman was just walking in his back door as Russ pushed the mower along their property line. Al waved hello, and Russ with his hands busy on the mower did that quick upward nod of the chin with a friendly smile which meant "Hi, good to see you." Al disappeared into his house as the mower rumbled by. Glad to see a friendly face and reminded too that Al and his wife, Joann, were just next door, real handy, Russ took note again of something to be thankful for this day—good neighbors.

Al and Joann Tillman had lived next door probably twenty years now—they raised their three kids and now it was just the two of them in that big house, not too much different from Russ and Lorraine, just younger by probably a dozen years. Heck of a nice couple, Russ thought, friendly and hard workers both of them and they kept a real tidy yard. Another mark in their favor, to Russ's way of thinking, was they had been steady customers at Fairway Foods, going back even to Al's parents, the Oscar Tillmans out on the farm north of town, who had been customers long before Russ took over the store from his dad. "Shoot, you can't beat neighbors like that," Russ always reminded Lorraine when the Tillman kids were teens and had an occasional loud party that lasted after the ten o'clock town whistle. "They're a good Morgan family."

But the neighbors on the other side, Russ couldn't speak of really. The Helvigs were fairly new to the block, probably just over a year now, a young couple with two small boys. They were friendly enough to mutter a "Hello" if he happened to catch them as they were going to or from the garage to the house, but they were not inclined to socialize anymore than that, quick to duck away out of sight. "Sour" was how Russ described them. Routinely some of the boys' toys spilled over into Russ and Lorraine's yard, and then Russ would return them to the side of the Helvig garage, lining them up in an orderly fashion, hoping to instill a standard of neighborhood neatness. Several times Russ even tried to make conversation with the older boy who was about school age, maybe get him to smile a little, but the boy had the same sullen look of his parents and only a blank stare when Russ told him, "You have some real nice toys—be sure to take good care of them and keep them in your yard." Made sense that their dog was antisocial too—a skinny little short-haired thing that yapped for no particular reason, straining at the leash on his spindly hind legs, his eyes frantic. Odd, Russ thought, that the neighbors before in that house, fussy and contrary Clem and Elvira Shuster, actually put an end to Russ and Lorraine's lab-terrier Matt when Matt got lose once too often and peed on their bushes. Elvira so much as predicted it when she told Russ one afternoon as he was leading Matt back to his kennel after chasing him for an hour, "Russel, you'd better watch out so that dog doesn't get into some serious trouble, running lose like that, relieving himself in other people's yards." And the morning Matt showed up real sick, laying there lifeless and foaming at the back door, old Elvira was watching from the window. She quickly ducked behind the curtain but not before Russ caught a glimpse of her. After that, Russ sensed a strangeness about that house, even after old Clem died and Elvira went off to live with her daughter in Wabasso, and the house sat empty for six months. And now the Helvigs.

"Yes, sirree, the Tillmans can't be beat for good neighbors," Russ thought again as he circled the mower near their tidy garden brimming with vegetables almost up to par with his own. Al's tomatoes never matched the size or quantity of Russ's, but he did have a knack for growing hot peppers, something Russ couldn't imagine eating anyway, but they sure were pretty to look at. "A garden like that says something about a person," Russ liked to tell Al those late summer evenings standing at the edge of Al's garden, comparing their harvests. "Working alongside Mother Nature, that's what gardening is all about—you've got to like the whole process, from planting to picking. Keeping it neat just sort of says you respect what old Mother Nature's given you—good seeds, good soil, and plenty of rain and sunshine, yes, sir."

"Yup, you're absolutely right, Russ, but I've never known anyone quite like you who likes picking the weeds as much as picking the harvest," Al would always say. "Gosh, I see you out there for hours on your knees, picking every gol-darned weed in sight. Joann will tell me, 'Get on out there now so Russ doesn't see all our weeds.'" Then Al would imitate his wife shaking her finger, and he and Russ would laugh. "But, Russel, the truth is: I just can't keep up with you. No, sir." Al didn't try to hide his admiration.

Russ thought about these things now as he cut a swath past his garden and then lapped the yard twelve more times, finishing the last stretch of grass there in the middle near the pear tree. He turned off the mower and stood in the shade of the small tree, wiping his forehead. So preoccupied he'd been with the exactness of the task and the stamina of pushing the clunky mower amidst the noise and fumes of it all, and now the pure pleasure of seeing the fresh mown grass, that the reality of his aloneness, the frailty of life really which had consumed his thoughts for a week now, was put on hold. Now looking over the trimmed yard, it was Lorraine's snap dragons planted next to the house that he noticed—colorful and swaying in the summer breeze in a carefree dance—and he remembered all the dark details all over again. If only he had more to mow.

He parked the mower back in its place in the garage and started to head for the house, eager for a drink of water. Just then Al reappeared from around the corner of the house with a smile and a wave of his hand, "Say, Russel, wait a minute, hold on a second . . ."

Russ turned to the familiar voice, his spirits taking an immediate lift just at the sound of his neighbor. "Well, hello again, Al—it's a little easier talking now without that loud mower. How are you doing?"

"Oh, me? Fine, fine, but it's you I'm concerned about, seeing you out there in the heat of the day mowing to beat the band. I tell you, now Joann will make me get out there too, just to keep up with your yard!" He grinned a wide, kind grin, careful not to be overly cheerful, considering Russ's new circumstances and this somewhat awkward first encounter after his good neighbor's loss.

Russ grinned back, and his eyes even lit up, "Heck, Al, you tell Joann that I'm trying to keep up with *you*—the way you two have your place so neat, always looking so nice and even trimmed around the trees and all those flowers—why, I should be working double time!" He wiped his forehead again and smiled. "But really, Al, don't get your mower out until it's cooled down a bit. I should have done that myself. The humidity today will get you, that's for sure." He adjusted his cap as he waited for a response, strangely running out of words today, at least the kind of words that wouldn't weigh a fellow down. "So what's up?"

Al's smile faded and his eyes shifted off to the distance. Just as Russ was about to fill in with another comment on the humidity or the yards, to avoid an uncomfortable lull in the conversation, Al looked back with determination, "Russel, that was a fine funeral you had for Lorraine and a good turnout too. Very nice."

Russ kept his eyes steady on Al despite the thud he felt in his stomach at the mention of funeral. He nodded and sighed. "Yes, Al, I thought so too—real nice. And the old preacher didn't get long-winded like with some, kept it short. Yeah, plenty warm out at the cemetery though, plenty warm. This time of year can get . . ."

"And just so you know, Russ—the reason that Joann and I didn't talk to you down there in the church basement was we could see that you were busy with all those relatives from out of town. We knew it was important for you to take time with them." Sounding all too much like a rehearsed speech, Al didn't pause for a breath or change his tone, and he didn't look Russ in the eye but instead off in the distance. "Well, anyway, Joann and I just want you to know that we're close by if you need us. You just holler if you need anything, anything at all. Just next door, you know." He gave a firm nod to affirm his commitment as he took a deep breath. Then he looked back at Russ.

"Well, that's real nice, Al . . ."

"Saw your daughter's car here the other morning. Yeah, we didn't want to bother when you had company. Lord knows, you've had lots going on, Russ." Al looked out at the vacant street. "Ah, has she gone home now?"

Even though Al's comments weren't much different from those dismal conversations in the church basement, Russ had a special tolerance today with his good neighbor. He had always liked Al, who not only was a heck of a friendly guy, but could fix a furnace too, which had come in handy over the years. One winter night a couple years ago when it was twenty below, Al came right over when Russ called him just after midnight telling him the furnace quit running. There was Al slogging through the snow drifts with his big overshoes and a hooded parka thrown on over his pajamas. He worked in the basement a good hour until the furnace clicked on again—didn't charge a dime for it either—said it was payment enough to have good neighbors like Russ and Lorraine, not to mention Russ giving all those garden tips.

"Yeah, sent her home," Russ said, not minding at all that Al had been keeping an eye on whose cars were and weren't in the neighborhood. "At first she wouldn't have it any other way—she wanted to stay a couple nights, probably even more. But heck, what can she do here?" The open-ended question went straight to Al, who could see he'd struck a nerve. Russ had thrown out his hands for emphasis.

"Well, Russ . . . ah . . . she could help you with . . ." Al hadn't prepared for this. He cleared his throat.

"Baby-sit me, like I'm some little kid? That's what it would amount to, and I've seen what that does. No sir, not for me. Don't you remember poor old Jake Johnson? Not worth a damn after his wife died!" Russ adjusted his cap again, folded his arms across his chest, and began tapping his index finger against his sleeve.

"Now, Russel, you know your girls just want to help you all they can. It's not easy for any of you." Al wanted to put his hand on Russ's shoulder but instead put both hands in his pockets and looked back to the ground as if the answer might be amongst the grass clippings. He kicked at a dandelion.

"I know, I know. I got good girls. It's just these first few days are the worst when everyone's wondering, 'Hey, how's this old duffer going to get along by himself? I sure don't need people wondering if this daughter or that one is going to help old Russel out." He paused, waiting for an encouraging word from Al, then thought better of it seeing that Al was still studying the ground. "Besides, that one has enough to take care of with her job and her family—and I know she helps with the farming too. She's a heck of a worker. No, Al, I told her to go ahead home where she belongs. I've got a lot to keep me busy. And the other two girls, they live so damned far away with families too. But, you know, Al, the way I see it, that's good for a guy to figure it out for himself! Like I say, I've got a lot to keep me busy." Now three of his fingers were tapping a drum roll.

"Ah huh, ah huh," Al was resting his chin in his hand, listening intently, amazed with his old neighbor's spunk, leaving no good argument for a guy like himself to challenge.

Russ recognized too that he had made his point. He rocked back on his heels. "Tell you what though, Al—I sure do appreciate having good neighbors like you and Joann. Yes, sir. It's good to have someone to chew the fat with, you know, and just like this here, you coming over like this—it's real nice. Just a simple talk like this, well, it can get a guy through a tough time and help to put all that bad stuff behind him—those hospitals and doctors—you know, all that bad stuff." Those last words felt bitter on his tongue.

Looking now at his neighbor, only middle-aged but already with a history of health problems, Russ saw an opening for his new personal campaign—warning unsuspecting patients, just like Lorraine, of the missteps ahead. "Come to think of it, Al, you're always going in to the Cities for those check-ups too—you'd better be sure to keep those yahoos on their toes." He pointed a finger at Al. "To think we made all those trips to the Cities, and Lorraine had tests until hell won't have it—and no one could figure anything out, not even the head of the whole works! He couldn't even give a guy a straight answer—not until it was too damned late, of course. That's the hell of it!" With that, Russ had his hands on his hips as if waiting for Al to offer a full explanation for the failed medical system.

Al, still with his chin in his hand, but wide-eyed now, nodded in agreement, knowing from experience to withhold comment until his friend finished. Russ wiped the sweat from his forehead again and sighed. "Yeah, that's the hell of it . . ." He rested one hand on the railing as he looked past Al and past his yard, to the cornfields bordering the end of town. "Always thought Lorraine and I would make it to fifty years for sure. Yup. Fifty, at least, that always seemed easy enough." His gaze turned back to Al. "Forty-eight, that's what it was, Al. Forty-eight . . . ."

Al dropped his long arms to his sides, shifted his weight and cleared his throat. "Forty-eight is pretty darned good, Russ. You and Lorraine had a good life, seems to me, raising those girls. You even making it through the war and all." Russ took note at his mention of the war, then looked up at the fluffy clouds and gave a nod, his jaw firm.

"I know, I know, Russ, it's not long enough though. It's never long enough. And you're absolutely right—those doctors need to be accountable. That's for darned sure." Russ was still studying the clouds, and Al took it as a cue to have his say.

"Joann and I knew that Lorraine must not have been feeling good for quite some time 'cause we didn't see her around in the yard this whole summer. Normally, she would have been out there watering her flowers—say, look at those snap dragons, how nice they still look. She'd like that." Russ gave a quick nod in the direction of the flowers as he waited for Al to finish. "Anyway, I know you mentioned every so often that she was laid up, and we didn't want to ask too much, you know, might think we were poking our nose into your business." Al noticed that Russ was focused now on the snap dragons. "But, yeah, you're right, Russ, about those doctors in the Cities. They're always too busy to talk to a guy more than a minute, then out the door they go on to the next poor guy, poof! Joann, she, of course, goes with me when I have my appointments—yeah, Joann, she . . ." Triggered by mentioning the name, Al looked at his watch mid-thought. "Gosh, Russel, almost forgot about the time! She says we can't be late for our granddaughter's birthday party—little Jesse, she turns one today, party is at five o'clock. We have to drive over to New Ulm so I'd better get going!"

Russ reacted too with the sudden change of topic. He looked at his own watch. "Ah, you're right, Al. I've got ten after five already so you'd better high-tail it. I don't want to be holding you up."

Al wheeled around, "Well, glad I caught you anyway . . ." He looked back over his shoulder and added as he hurried off, "You take good care of yourself, Russ. And remember, Joann and I are just next door. Be seeing you now . . ." He waved.

"You bet, Al." Russ trailed after his neighbor a few steps to the corner of the house. "Good talkin' to you too. You and Joann have a good time . . ." he spoke out as he watched Al walk back across the yard. He especially noticed a slight limp and a bit of a slump in Al's lean shoulders. "Hmm, we're all getting older," he mulled and then turned to go into the house, oddly refreshed by the conversation.

But the empty house had a staleness to it as if it had been closed up over the summer, and it was uncomfortably quiet, the kind of quiet that sounded sad. Strange, Russ thought, how even in these last months when Lorraine stayed in the recliner all day, not moving much or making a sound really, the house still had a rhythm to it. When he'd walk into the quiet house, he'd know that she was there. "Lorraine, it's me, I'm home," he'd holler in a sing-song way so as not to startle her in case she'd be asleep and not hear the door. Now there were just tell-tale signs of her.

He plugged in the fan on top of the refrigerator and stood at the kitchen sink as he downed a tall glass of water. The whir of the fan sounded just right, filling the empty air. He compared his watch with the kitchen clock, confirming again that it was already late in the afternoon, normally when Lorraine would be in the kitchen starting supper. He imagined the sounds of clanging pans, chopping, cupboard doors opening and closing, opening and closing. Shaking away the thought, he walked into the living room where he pulled the west curtains to shut out the hot afternoon sun. He sat down in his recliner, turned on the television, and flipped channels until he landed on a re-run of "Hee Haw," one of the few shows that Lorraine enjoyed. As a country group crooned and fiddled, he leaned back, closed his eyes, and drifted off.

But the volume at station break startled him so that he twitched and then half-listened to the commercial for New Horizons, a housing opportunity opening soon in New Ulm. The sales woman in her overly-cheery voice spoke about "active seniors looking for a social environment in their golden years." He growled and shifted position. "Right," he mumbled, "active seniors." And those golden years, well, they're not so hot, if you ask me." Until now this sort of "housing opportunity" seemed anything but for someone like himself and Lorraine, comfortably situated in their home of forty-eight years. The unsettling thought of going it alone now hung on like indigestion as the commercial played out. He shifted again, to turn his good ear away from the sound.

And then, like a bit of magic coming right out of the television, a sports announcer came on with a particularly bright commanding voice, and overly loud as if he was speaking to an audience of one: Russ Albrecht. Russ turned and opened one eye just a peek. "Stay tuned for Twins Baseball tonight—coverage starts at six-thirty right here on WCCO. It's the Twins and Detroit in the Dome. Don't miss it!" Russ checked his watch, then took a deep breath, closed his eyes, and thanked the good Lord again.

CHAPTER 5
DAILY SPECIALS

As Russ walked into Shelly's pool hall, the jingle of the old door sounded particularly friendly, like the banter of an old buddy. The establishment dated back to the early 1900s, and even though the pool tables had been gone for most of the years and replaced by more lucrative dining tables, the business thrived, serving breakfast and lunch to the locals. Russ had been coming to this place since his first job slaughtering chickens at the Produce, which was just next door and across the alley then. That's when he was just out of high school, back in 1928.

The air was smoky as usual, and although Russ gave up the cigarette habit twenty years ago, he still liked the smell. He associated the thick tobacco air with guys getting together for coffee and small talk like here in this little café over the many years. And his senses carried him back to the war too when all the GIs smoked, especially when they were on a rest and waiting for their next orders. The soldiers passed the time with cards and smokes—somehow the deep draws on a Lucky Strike quelled the dark thoughts of an uncertain next day, a day in harm's way. So now he welcomed that smell.

The pool hall was noisy with chatter and laughs, the stacking of plates and silverware and the whirring of the exhaust fans over the grills. All the tables were full with the usual farmers and their farmhands who had come in from the fields for their noon meal. Old Elmer Bendixen was in a lively discussion with his two boys, now running the farmstead, Russ had heard. Sitting there too was Hubert Iffert and a couple of others from the Farmers' Elevator Board. The stools at the counter were filled with several of the local merchants and a couple of what looked like out-of-town guys, with matching shirts and caps from Northern States Power. Russ spotted an empty stool at the counter in the back and headed for it, straightening his posture a bit and picking up his step, a quickness he was known for.

He would have been noticed just as one of the regulars had it been mid-morning on any other weekday. That would be for coffee, or coffee and a roll if Shelly had a batch of cinnamon rolls fresh out of the oven. But the noontime scene with its daily specials and full menu was brand new to him, the kind of experience he might expect on a family road trip somewhere in Nebraska. Then a guy might lower his food expectations to restaurant fare, just to offset the adventure of getting away to see new territory. But on an everyday basis, well, restaurants were, in Russ's opinion anyway, good for coffee and rolls. Period. Even with Lorraine working part time at the nursing home these past ten years, she drove home each day to cook a noon meal for the two of them. As with most people living a comfortable life like this, humming along day-to-day, Russ never questioned his good fortune. Sharing a life had a lot of built-in advantages, he was learning—like home cooking.

He noticed a few heads turn as he walked by. "Say, Russ!" Someone grabbed his arm. He turned to see Einar Thorwald, a farmer who every year about this time invited him to hunt ducks on his slough, just three miles out of Morgan on the east road. And Einar and his wife were in the couples' Whist group with Russ and Lorraine for the last ten years. "How are you doing? Sure glad to see you around again!" Einar had a robust face with a wide, easy smile revealing yellowed teeth from years of chewing tobacco. He held out his hand.

"Yeah, good to see you too, Einar!" Just like that solid feeling when he talked to his neighbor Al, he felt anchored again—anchored with his feet set on good Morgan soil, or in this case, a good Morgan establishment. He darned-well respected someone who would reach out like this to bring him back into the fold of everyday living. That's what he thought now as he responded with an extra firm handshake. "Yes, sir, good to see you!" But, hoping to keep the conversation on the light and short side to avoid slipping into more talk of dark topics and just plain not wanting to lose his seat at the counter, he glanced there again and motioned over his shoulder. "I'm just heading over to that stool over there—ah, looks like the last one too. Thought I'd check out what kind of grub they have here for dinner. Heard it's pretty good. Never tried one of those 'daily specials' I see there on the board." He smiled like he was a new guy in town.

Einar kept a tight hold of Russ's hand to reinforce what he needed to convey, his eyes turning serious now with his brow furrowed. "You know, Russ, the wife and I were very sorry to hear about Lorraine." He paused, peering over his glasses and still holding tight to Russ's hand. Einar's strong hand, muscular and rough, told that he was a long-time farmer. "We're sure going to miss her. Yeah, that sure is tough for you, losing her like that." He zeroed in close. "And we want you to know that we couldn't get to the funeral because we were out of town at my brother's place up north by Milaca, helping him winterize his resort, you know—heck of a job it was too. But Edna, she's been worrying about not getting to the funeral and wondering what you're thinking of us—you know, not being there. She put our memorial in the mail yesterday, so you'll be getting that." He squeezed Russ's hand before letting go.

"Well, to tell you the truth, Einar, I can't really say right offhand who was and who wasn't there—it all went so fast. So you tell Edna not to worry. And, ah, as for something in the mail, well, that's real nice of you two . . ." Russ put his hands in his pockets. He was stuck now on just what to say next, with the mention of a memorial. How the money would be spent—these were details he still needed to discuss with the daughters. A slight change of subject seemed reasonable. ". . . Yeah, Lorraine loved to get a bunch together for cards and coffee, that's for sure. The house had to be just-so, though, nothing out of place, and everything spic and span." He tried one of those cheerful laughs, but cleared his throat instead mid-way.

Einar was eager to pick up. "Oh, those gals and their cleaning— you know, Edna already started in on that for the group coming this Friday, and she . . ." His eyes popped open wide at his obvious mis- step in bringing up future Whist groups—the same old group, minus Russ and Lorraine, that is. "Oh gosh, Russ, didn't mean to mention that. But, oh, what the heck, maybe you should know that the Jensens are going to take your place, you know Cletus and Eleanor . . ." Einar scratched the back of his head, and Russ just smiled and nodded.

"Yeah, well anyway, what I want to say, Russ, is we just want you to know that if there's anything you need, anything at all, don't be afraid to speak up. Edna, she's planning to bring over a meal for you one of these days." He scratched his head again, coming up with another thought. "And you know, Russ, you can always get a meal at Gil-Mor. I heard that it kind of livens up the day for those residents to see someone come in and eat with them, you know. Some of them are still pretty good, you know with their minds, so a guy can even get to talking with them too, pass the time—I heard a guy can even go out and play cards there, Thursdays, I think, it is. You might think about doing that, Russ." Einar looked proud of his uplifting suggestion. "Well, anyway, Russ, if there's anything we can do . . ."

Russ sighed at the notion that the nursing home might be the place to catch a meal or a little socializing, and that his friend here might even think that this was a reasonable option. Einar was just like all the others with their memorials and casseroles, trying to come up with the right words. Russ bit his lip and just shrugged. "Thanks, Einar, but that's the heck of it. What can anyone do about it? Dying is just part of life, that's all—we just pick up and carry on. Yup, just a part of life, Einar, just a part of life." Russ liked that he could boldly come out with the word "dying" just like that. His teeth clenched but not that Einar would notice.

Russ paused, seeing Einar nod in agreement almost like in a trance. "F-o-r-t-y—e-i-g-h-t years," Russ drew the number out as if Einar needed to lip read, "that's how long we were married, Einar. Forty-eight. That's a heck of a long time." He paused again so that Einar might add something hopeful. Resting back on his heels and with his hands still in his pockets, Russ didn't shift his eyes off Einar, holding him to the fire.

But Einar really couldn't muster anything to say. He took off his Morgan Elevator cap to scratch his forehead, revealing a tan line just above his eyebrows. His gaze dropped to the floor.

"Like I said, Einar—don't you worry about me. I'm getting along okay, but thank you anyway. I've got plenty to stay busy, that's for sure—you know, my job, the garden, plus every gol-darn board in town, a heck of a lot of stuff. And I've got the daughters too. Heck, they're always calling now—I can't even take a nap without the telephone ringing." He faked a chuckle. "Yeah, I've got a lot going on . . ." Russ leaned back and began to jingle the keys in his pocket.

Einar still apparently was mulling this over, still with his eyes to the floor.

Russ sensed the notion that now might be a good time to add some helpful advice for someone like Einar. Here was Einar, sitting pretty with his present circumstances: his farming business on an even keel and a wife to share whatever might come along life's way. "Tell you what you can do though, Einar," Russ sounded more like he was offering up a deal. "You and your wife, you've still got each other. You'd better appreciate what you've got, that's for sure."

Einar looked up.

"Yes, sir, Einar, you'd better thank the good Lord every day for what you've got. All those years together. When a guy's got his health, he's a rich man. Darn it, life's too short!" Russ felt a slight catch in his throat and a sting in his eyes as he said the word "short," throwing him off-guard. So he exaggerated a cough.

Einar sighed and fiddled with the bill of his cap not noticing. "Isn't that so . . ." He hung on the word while his eyes shifted to a blank stare off to another place, someplace other than the pool hall on another day. That place happened to be the emergency room in Redwood Falls where Einar was just that very week after a scare with chest pains when he was baling hay. After four hours of tests, he was sent home with a change in his heart medicine and a warning to take it easy or he could expect more of those angina pains, sobering advice he'd rather not dwell on. "Isn't that so . . . Yeah, life is short, Russ . . . real short . . ."

Then, out of the din of the restaurant like a wake-up call, Shelly from behind the counter hollered, "Order's up!" As if she had snapped her fingers to break the trance, Einar stood tall again, glanced at his watch, and put his cap back on with determination, "Well, Russ, I've got to be heading out now, got to get back to the farm. Knut's boy is coming over to help me finish up the baling this week. Sure was good talking to you though, Russel. I'll be sure to tell Edna what you said." He leaned close then with a sly grin and whispered, "Say, you might try the pork chops—they're especially good today. And sometimes Shelly runs out so you'd better hurry." He winked.

"Ah . . . sure!" Russ had perked up too and felt better for the change to lighter conversation. "The pork chops . . . okay, I just might. Hmm, runs out, you say?"

Einar nodded and smiled wide, revealing those yellow teeth again. "Yup, runs out sometimes. See you around, Russ. Oh, and say—it's just a couple weeks now before duck season, and you know you're always welcome at our place. Remember now . . ." he pointed at Russ, "I'll expect to see you!" Einar squeezed Russ's arm again, tipped his cap and turned for the door.

"Thanks, Einar. Now *that* I'll remember!" Russ unconsciously smiled as the door jingled and Einar walked out. Russ stood and watched for a second while the door closed, his thoughts now skipping by the heaviness of this summer day to cool autumn weather and duck blinds, like changing channels. "Well, how about that—an invitation to hunt—now that's what a guy needs!"

The waitress was already waiting with her pencil and pad, when Russ made it back to the stool at the counter. "Saw you eyeing this seat, Russ, so I shooed a couple away already. Told 'em it was saved. Besides, looked like you needed to chat a minute there with Einar." It was Shelly's crusty mother, Dorothy, helping out today. She had turned the business over to Shelly and her husband a few years ago after a bout with exhaustion from the restaurant business and looking after her own invalid husband. But now she gladly helped her daughter at a minute's notice, knowing it was always an opportunity to soak in the latest Morgan news. Nothing got by Dorothy. No one ever quite understood how Dorothy raised such a sweet, mild mannered daughter as Shelly, and a good cook besides but, no matter, the two worked seamlessly in the restaurant.

"Gee thanks, Dorothy. Let me see here. I'll order something real quick since you've been waiting." He looked up at the menu on the chalkboard just below a mounted deer head on the wall and next to a giant mirror with "Hamm's Beer, Land of Sky Blue Waters" in blue script lettering across the top. The chalkboard read: "Pork chops, mashed potatoes, corn & coffee $3.00—Sloppy Joe, chips & coffee $2.50—Homemade apple pie $1.00."

"Well, that's an easy decision—I'll have the pork chop dinner, if I'm not too late. I heard it's 'especially' good."

"Not too late, Russ! And excellent choice!"

"Oh, and my coffee with plenty of cream, please."

"You bet, Russ. Coming right up." She pivoted on her toes and, with the efficiency only a waitress of some forty years might achieve, she whisked off to turn in the order, retrieved dirty dishes from the counter on her way, and just that quickly returned with a cup of coffee and two creamers, along with a piece of pie for old Verne Otto, several stools down from Russ. "There, that'll get you started, Russel."

There at the counter, Russ settled in with his cup of coffee, sitting next to Gordy the barber, and next to him, Vernon, a farmer from out south of town. After the obligatory condolences for which this time he put forth an honest, gracious effort, he was relieved that the conversations abruptly turned to the price of hogs and what that in turn might mean for the cost of a hair cut these days. Vernon, who also did his time in the war, moved the conversation then to the ever-increasing financial troubles of the VFW and the dwindling membership in the last several years. "The old duffers are kicking off, that's why!" That's what Russ blurted out, but then he sat back and mostly listened, oddly content just to soak up familiar everyday life at the counter of the pool hall.

So comfortable and relaxed he was now, he might have stayed long after finishing his last bite of potatoes, but the crowd was thinning until he was the only one remaining at the counter. The last table with several young farmhands Russ didn't know by name, was just settling up their bills. In just another hour, the place would be filling up again with afternoon card games over coffee and pie, just before closing time at three o'clock.

He straightened his walk and gave a nod to the guys at the table as he headed to the door, and Shelly, who up until then had been busy at the grill and now was wiping off the counter, made a special point to holler after him, "Thanks for coming in, Russ!" Dorothy waved with a cigarette between her fingers, as she cleared a table, "You take care, Russel. Our special tomorrow will be fried chicken."

CHAPTER 6
BOUNTIFUL HARVEST

Russ knocked on the door and then busied himself whistling under his breath as he stood waiting on the cement steps, noticing the wear and tear on the house that sat across the street from him all these years. Funny, he thought, how from his front porch the house didn't really look like it was in need of repair. What he had noticed instead was the steady stream of family in and out of that door over the years. Del and Ruth Swenson had eleven kids he knew for sure; then he stopped counting. "Good Catholics." That's how he and Lorraine and all the other Protestants in town liked to refer to the large, ever-expanding families that attended St. Michael's. Protestants in Morgan generally kept their distance from the Catholics. Del was the town cop for years and years, and Ruth just kept having kids. When they built the house back in the fifties, the money must have run out so they stopped after the basement was finished and lived in that for several years before tackling any more of the project. A "basement house" is how he explained it to his own small girls when they questioned why the house where the Swenson kids lived looked different, even scary—almost flat to the ground except for a triangular section jutting up which enclosed the stairs, all covered in a black tar paper. Then early one spring, Del and his two oldest sons began to put up studs for the first floor and by the end of that summer, the house blended in with the other small-frame houses on the block. Now, a couple of decades later, the Swenson kids were out on their own, but they all stayed in the area and congregated at this little house often as if it was a family magnet, bringing along their girlfriends and boyfriends, and then of course their new families. One of the girls even became a nun. How they all fit, Russ wondered, and the house didn't even have a porch.

The inside door opened, and Ruth's smiling round face greeted Russ through the screen. She had a large mixing bowl clutched on her hip as she swung open the screen door and held it with her other hand, "Well, hello, Russel. Come on in. Come on in. That wind out of the west is a little cool today, quite a change from our summer weather." Her voice was so cheery and the energy surrounding her so pure and infectious that Russ felt a surge in optimism at just that moment as he took it all in. "Ah, yes . . . hi there, Mrs. Swenson!" he said a little surprised at himself for sounding like a door-to-door salesman, after a lifetime of living just across the street.

He stepped inside, but just far enough to convey that he intended for his visit to be short, to just drop off the bag, really. "I sure don't want to interrupt anything . . . you look awfully busy . . ."

"No, no, I'm just baking something for the 'Sharing' project at church tomorrow night—a big drive to collect items for the needy. I'm the chairman now so I'd better come with a treat for all my faithful volunteers—they expect it!" She beamed as she slid her glasses back further on her nose and resumed stirring the mixture in the bowl. "Now what can I do for you, Russel?"

"Well, I just want to give you some things from my garden, that's all." Russ held the bag front and center. "Now just speak up if you can't use this stuff . . . " Looking into the bag, he pointed to the items, "Let me see, there's some carrots, broccoli, and a real big cabbage in here. Got too much for me to eat, that's for darned sure." He held out the bag so she could look inside. "Ah . . . I see you have your hands full, so just tell me where to put it . . . .maybe there on the kitchen table?" Looking into the kitchen he could see the countertop was covered with baking supplies and dirty dishes. Heavy-looking boxes were stacked in the corner, each labeled "Sharing." A toddler was busy playing with pots and pans on the kitchen floor. "You've got a helper there, too, I see."

Ruth laughed, "Yes, he's quite a helper, that's my youngest grandson, James, youngest temporarily, I should say—Anna is expecting in March and Mark's wife in May." She stepped into the kitchen and cleared a space on the counter for her mixing bowl. "Here, I'll just take that bag so I can see what goodies you have in there. "Oh, my . . . ," she peeked into the bag and sniffed, "hmm, I love that smell of garden." She threw her head back with her eyes closed, savoring the aromatic blend of fresh vegetables as though it were intoxicating.

Russ wasn't accustomed to theatrics like this, especially considering the ordinary items and considering his ordinary neighbor, so he didn't know how to respond. But he couldn't help but smile, which he noticed felt very good.

Ruth opened her eyes and with her own broad smile looked back at Russ. "This is such a treat, Russel, thank you very much. Of course, we will use every bit! Everyone knows that you have the very best garden in Morgan. For heaven sake, you could win a ribbon at the state fair, I'm sure of it." She turned and pointed to the window out back. "Oh, of course, my little patch does all right, except I just run out of space. And now it's done-for already this year." She turned back to the bag. "My, this is quite a treat!" She lifted out the heavy cabbage with both hands and admired it like a work of art. "Wait 'til I tell Del about this cabbage . . . he loves cooked cabbage!"

Russ couldn't help but settle back to soak in all of Ruth's exuberance, not just for his produce, but for all of life it seemed. Little James by now wanted to see in the bag too so he was holding onto his grandma's pant leg, pulling at her sweater. Ruth set the bag on the table and picked him up. "Look in here, James—see what Mr. Albrecht brought for us?"

Russ smiled and turned to leave. "Well, I'll get out of your way now—just wanted to bring this stuff over while it's still good and fresh. Seems like the garden really produced this year, so I'm glad to have places for it all to go. Next year I won't be planting much, if anything. In fact, think I'll just cover it with grass and be done with it." He started for the door.

"Oh, goodness, don't do that, Russel! You have a gift for gardening! The Good Lord gave it to you!"

Russ shook his head. "Naw, just good black dirt, that's all." He smiled and waved her off as he opened the door.

She had followed close after him. "Thank you so much again, Russel, but wait a minute . . ." Russ felt a gentle touch on his shoulder. "You took me by such surprise with these wonderful vegetables that I haven't even asked how you are getting along—you being all alone now." Ruth creased her brow, her eyes turning sad. "That's got to be tough, especially after such a long, blessed life together like you had with Lorraine." Ruth had such a reverence about her, and even a glow as she stood in the doorway facing the afternoon sun. For a second, Russ sensed he might be talking to an angel, at least someone a notch or two above himself. He was feeling guiltier by the second for earlier slipping in that word "darned."

Inspired too at the thought of being "blessed," he hesitated for the right words. "Oh, I'm getting along just fine. But you know, you're absolutely right about being, how you put it, 'blessed.'" He raised a finger to his chin. "In fact, that's the way I'm going to look at it, Mrs. Swenson . . . er . . . Ruth—blessed." And with that, Russ turned and proceeded down the steps. "I've got more to deliver so I'll be on my way." He waved back to little James.

Ruth called after him, "The good Lord will watch out for you, Russel. Just wait and see. He always provides."

Russ looked back to smile and wave again.

Those words would come back to Russ more than a few times over the next several years, and he pondered them now as he walked back across the street to his house to pick up the other bag of vegetables. It wasn't as if this was news to him, the idea that the good Lord watches out and provides. For goodness sake, he had firsthand knowledge of that back in the war, living proof, he liked to think. The truth though was that he had forgotten about it these past forty years—well, not actually forgotten, considering he told and re-told the stories of getting through the war to any eager listener—but it was more like he hadn't availed himself of that comforting notion since his days on the frontline of battle. "This is as good a time as any to be reminded," he vowed now as he set the bag of vegetables on the seat next to him and then backed out of his driveway on his second delivery.

Roy finally appeared at the door but only after Russ had knocked loudly a half a dozen times and was reaching in his pocket for the house key. "Oh, Russel! Good to see you!" Roy pushed open the door.

"Gosh, darn it, Roy, I was getting worried for a second there and thought I'd better let myself in . . . maybe you were having another spell. But looks like maybe you were just napping huh?"

Roy quickly smoothed the sides of his graying, sandy hair and rubbed his eyes. "You betcha I was napping, Russel," and he yawned. "Ah, how many times did you knock?" He stepped to the side holding the door so Russ could step by.

"Oh, just enough to get your attention, Roy, and probably the whole neighborhood too!" He patted Roy on the shoulder and smiled as he continued on through the matchbox-sized living room to the kitchen area where he set the bag down on the counter. Roy tagged behind.

"What you got there, Russel?"

"Oh, some good stuff out of my garden . . . you see here on top the last of my tomatoes . . . those you can just slice and eat, of course. 'Beefsteak' they're called." He carefully set out two large tomatoes. "Then there's some carrots, which I know you like to eat raw, and they keep real good, 'Nantes Coreless' is what I plant every year. See here, I've got them all cleaned and separately bagged for the refrigerator." He pulled out the plastic bag. "And you can boil a potato, right? Even a bachelor like you can do that."

Roy nodded, up on his toes to view the contents.

"I threw in some of these big Yukons and then some of the small reds." Russ reached in the bag and brought out a perfectly formed golden-white potato as big as his fist and held it up to view all sides. "Darned good luck with the potatoes this year, I'll have to say that. Got my root cellar stocked." He put the potato back in the bag and stood there with his hands on his hips, satisfied, waiting for a reaction.

"Well, gosh, Russel, this is real nice." Roy's eyes were open wide with wonder. "After running into you at the post office, I was just looking forward to you stopping by, you know, to check on my mail and so forth—didn't expect something like this." He rubbed his chin and smiled, proud of having a visitor. "Yup, you're right, potatoes are one of the things I can cook—the other is eggs." Eager to prove his point, he reached for a blackened pan on a small shelf over the stove. "See here, this is my pot for boiling stuff. Otherwise, I have my cereals, you know, which come in real handy . . . and of course crackers with some liverwurst or bologna, that sort of thing." He was pleased with his self-sufficiency as he pointed to the two large cereal boxes at the corner of the counter, Puffed Wheat and Frosted Flakes, next to a tin of saltines. "I get by pretty good." He gave a wide grin and firm nod of his chin as confirmation.

Russ had been in this kitchen before, sitting at the table with Roy working on everything from bills and insurance forms to the Last Will and Testament of Roy E. Hanson, but never had he really considered how Roy got by day to day, food-wise. Looking around the minimal kitchen now, he suddenly saw himself. Maybe not today, or next week, but definitely somewhere down the line, he would be looking at a box of cold cereal thinking he was getting by "pretty good." He dismissed the thought.

"You bet you do, Roy! Yeah, looks like you've got everything a guy could ever need. Always said you have it real nice and convenient here too, everything pretty much within reach." That last part certainly was true, Russ thought, as he reached out his arms to demonstrate the efficiency of really only needing to pivot around to work at the counter or the stove or to reach the refrigerator. "And only a couple of steps and you're right there with your TV and recliner. Best part is you don't have much to clean!" Russ felt a particular warmth in seeing Roy's big smile.

"You betcha, Russ."

"Well, anyway . . ." Russ reached in the bag again and this time brought out two of the red potatoes, "like I said, it was a heck of a good year for potatoes. Just thought you might like a few. I certainly won't be planting much next year—think I'll just cover it with grass and be done with it." At that, he looked over his glasses at Roy for a reaction.

"What's that you say—done with it?" Roy put his hand over his mouth and chuckled. "Naw, Russel, . . . you know better than that." He emphasized those last words. Roy was all too familiar with the phrase because Russ used it every time Roy put himself down. Now Roy got a kick out of using it too, not often the one to rally another. "Yeah, you know better than that, Russel."

"Hah!" Russ returned the potatoes to the bag and with a crisp fold set it on the counter. "You just wait and see, Roy . . . it will be *grass* next year. Yup, nice and easy—I'll just mow it all down!"

Roy just shook his head and rubbed his chin with a knowing smile. But before he could come up with some convincing reasons for a garden, he could see that Russ was off to another topic. As if in his own kitchen, Russ began clearing an area at the table, moving the butter dish and salt and pepper to the side with a newspaper and a stack of coupons, along with some loose change, a couple pieces of hard candy, and a clipping of the Twins Baseball schedule, which caught Russ's eye enough to mentally note the next game. "Well, let's get to work here, Roy! Let's look at your bills and whatever you need done. I know you have a lot saved up over the past few weeks, with me not around much and busy with . . . you know . . . all those doctors visits . . . you know, for Lorraine." Russ cleared his throat as he took off his jacket and cap, setting them on the recliner. He pulled back a kitchen chair and sat down at the table, taking out a pen and pad from his shirt pocket and folding his hands on the table, waiting. His thumbs circled one way, then the other.

"Oh, gosh, you're right about that, Russel! I've got lots for you to look at!" Roy seemed to jump in his shoes as he switched gears to the business at hand and the real reason for Russ' visit . . . those financial matters and paper work too detailed and complicated for someone like himself, impaired along those lines since the stroke. His explanation to the guys at the pool hall was always, "I'm not too quick with the head stuff anymore," and then he'd chuckle, as if he'd told a good joke. "Now take Russel. He'd go on proudly, "he's my numbers guy—he keeps me on the straight and narrow." Fact was, this help with numbers enabled Roy to maintain his independent living status, there alone in that tiny house.

With his usual limp, Roy hurried off to the bedroom as Russ continued to twiddle his thumbs, now with an impatient whistle to fill the time. "Just a second, Russel—that's all I need to find the stuff . . . got it all ready for you . . ." Russ could hear the shuffling of papers, then a muffled, ". . . somewhere here on the dresser . . . ah, here it all is!" Roy returned to the table with two bundles of mail, each rubber-banded, and a checkbook. "Here, I got them separated like you told me, Russel. Bills and then the other stuff." He set the bundles in front of Russ and handed him the checkbook, proud like a student.

"Good, good. Hmm, looks like you sorted out all the junk too . . ."

"Yup, just like you said."

Russ tilted his head back as he refocused through his bifocals to review the bank register. "Ah, huh . . ."

Roy looked on. "It's okay? I only wrote that one check for cash like you told me, you know, when you were going to be gone at the hospital with your wife."

"Looks just fine, Roy. Ah, huh . . . Now let's take a look at these bills."

Roy took a deep breath and nodded in satisfaction as Russ opened the first bill.

"Let's see . . . Morgan Oil Company, $50.00 . . . says here 'tank filled September 1st' . . . well, that's a good reminder that fall is here, don't you think, Roy?" Not waiting for an answer, he rattled on, "Yeah, gotta keep that tank filled to have heat, that's for sure. Gotta have heat here in Minnesota, by golly. Okay, let's get that one paid!" As Russ wrote out the check with a flourish, he expounded on the rising heat costs and his own personal back-up system if ever his furnace should fail, a woodstove in his basement. Sitting pretty with a whole wall of cut wood, perfectly dried and ready to use from his ten acres down in the valley, that woodstove, he loved to say, was "the best investment I ever made. Picked it up just after the war."

"Yeah, you've got a real good back-up there, Russel, with that wood stove of yours."

"You bet I do." Russ licked the envelope. "Okay, next one . . ."

Roy pulled out a chair for himself but then just hovered instead. "I know . . . I'll make us some coffee!" He hoped that Russ would have a story for every one of those bills at the table, and a cup of coffee might just make that happen. He got busy setting a pan of water on the stove, then retrieved two mugs from the sink, swished them out, and spooned a heaping portion of instant coffee granules into each.

Russ scratched out some numbers on his note pad, figuring Roy's doctor visits and medications since his last spell in the spring. "I come up with only $25.00 that you owe, Roy—your insurance should pay the rest of it!" He looked up at Roy with a satisfied smile.

Roy smiled too. He served up the steaming black coffee, and the two sat there at the kitchen table for the next couple of hours as Russ worked through the bills, insurance notices, and then finally a bank statement, all the while filling in stories to embellish an otherwise dreary task.

That evening just before sunset, as Russ walked out to his garage to empty the trash, he stopped when a movement out by the garden caught his eye. But it was just a neighborhood cat slinking through the backyard. As he watched the cat disappear behind the rhubarb, Russ couldn't help but take in the rich colors cast by the low sun. The soft maroon and yellow of the dried marigolds along the garden edge against the striking blackness of the clumps of earth turned for another season was a beauty that struck to his core. He set down the bag of trash, walked to the garden and began to plot his crops for next spring.

CHAPTER 7
THE HOTDISH

That's the way it went for Russ the next few weeks—coping by staying busy, tending to business, getting things done. He sat now at his kitchen table staring at an imposing Pyrex dish on the counter, sealed with aluminum foil, the contents frozen solid from a month in the freezer, and he pondered life's inequities. He had filled his days, but his days left him empty.

Now too with the approach of fall, some of that busy work was played out. The garden was laid to rest. The yard was dormant. Even fall fishing and hunting offered only short-lived pleasures. His Kenmore freezer, well-stocked with ducks and geese and walleye filets, didn't give him even half the satisfaction he had hoped.

Church didn't offer much either in the way of lifting a guy's spirits. Those first few Sundays after the funeral and as matter of routine from the past forty-eight years, Russ showed up at St. John's Lutheran. He sat in that pew where he and Lorraine always sat, midway on the right side and next to the aisle. But given his bad ear and the new preacher's habit of slurring, Russ didn't make out much of the sermon. Hoping to feel connected again, even to catch a hint of mercy, instead he left with an uncomfortable resentment and headache, not the kind of outcome you want from church. From then on, Russ parked himself in his recliner each Sunday morning, tuned in to televised church services direct from sunny Sacramento, California, with palm trees next to the altar. Dr. Schuller's motivational messages came through loud and clear, and the hour always included musical productions, very similar, he thought, to the Lawrence Welk programs he and Lorraine had enjoyed. Still, the church service lasted only so long and so too with the motivational message for the week. He stared at the Pyrex dish.

And for even the cheeriest, the shorter days at summer's end always bring a melancholy mood in Minnesota where the long winter ahead threatens like a lock-down. Although not one to dwell on effects of a simple season change, still, this year Russ took special note of the lower sun and the longer nights. He found himself down in the mouth, not at all his usual take on life. And the heck of it was he had never even once imagined himself alone in this kitchen. Life's inequities.

This was the state of things, his life after Lorraine, now as he sat at the kitchen table staring at the Pyrex dish. He noticed condensation starting to appear on the foil. Glancing at the clock, Russ realized an hour had slipped by. At attention now, he planned . . . suppose a guy could just let that thing thaw for the day and then about five o'clock toss it in the oven and see what turns out. A guy might have an appetite for it by then anyway. Half curious now about the contents, he got up from the table to peek under the foil —sure enough, looked like slices of potatoes, which was enough to lift his mood.

Ready to move on with the day, he reached in his shirt pocket for a notepad and pen and began jotting down a to-do list:

1. Send estate tax forms to Uncle Sam for Jensen estate,

2. Tidy up basement,

3. Check in on Roy—make sure he ordered more gas for furnace,

4. Double-check <u>my</u> fuel tank . . . .

He paused, looking back at item three, and then with a glint in his eye, said out loud, "Hey, wait a minute!" Russ stood up and turned to look again at the Pyrex dish—as if addressing it, he said Roy's name, dragged-out in a singsong: "R-o-y H-a-n-s-o-n . . . Ah, hah . . . ah, hah . . . poor old Roy Hanson, all by himself too . . . I just bet he could use some company, and *he* might like to give that dish a try!" Russ reached for the phonebook.

"Yeah, Roy? This is Russ. How's it going today?"

"Oh, Russel! Yeah, well . . . good, good . . . can't complain. How 'bout you?" He sounded tired.

"Just fine, Roy . . . just fine. Say, what I'm calling about is . . . well, I've got a hotdish here thawing out, one that a daughter brought over right after the funeral. It's more than I can eat by myself, that's for darned sure. I was wondering if you wanted to come over around suppertime and help me out with it? Can't guarantee how it'll taste, but the daughter's a good cook. And if you know some other guy who might be needing some supper, well, there's a heck of lot here." It was as if he couldn't get the words out fast enough.

"A hotdish?" Roy's voice had raised a pitch. "You say you have plenty . . . and then-some, huh?" He chuckled. "My ma used to say 'then-some' when she had cooked a big batch. Yeah, I always got a kick out of that, yes sir . . ."

"So, what do you think . . . give it a try?"

"Well, gosh, yeah . . . I sure will be there, Russ! I've always liked a good hotdish. I know ma made lots of 'em, and I liked every one of 'em—real good food growing up. I remember she would throw together . . ."

"Well, good then. And how about some other guy who might take a notion? I for sure don't want any leftovers . . . it's the 'then-some,' like you say, that worries me." Russ enjoyed that Roy was easy to amuse, and with this comment, Roy didn't disappoint.

"Oh, Russel . . . I might eat more than you think, being it's a good, old, hotdish!"

"Well, I know it's old, that's for sure—been in my freezer 'bout two months. I just don't know how good it is."

Roy couldn't contain himself with the exchange of one-liners. "Hold on just a second, Russel . . ." He set the receiver down on the table so that he could blow his nose. "That's pretty funny, Russel—old and good! But what's that you say? Invite another guy? Hmmm."

"Well, there's got to be some other guy around town who's sitting around like us on our duffs, waiting for a meal."

"Hmmm . . . my gosh, you know . . . Richard Frederiksen, now he's one who is always looking for something to do. His wife's been gone over a year. Oh, once in a while he picks me up and we get a hamburger downtown. Let's see, it's about 1:30 now, so I'll bet you he's . . . well, I bet he's at the pool hall playing cards, if you want to try him there . . . yup, I'm pretty sure that's where you might find him."

"Richard Frederiksen? Hmm . . ." Russ only knew Richard Frederiksen really just enough to say hello, and that was usually at the pool hall. Once or twice they might have been at the same table playing cards, that sort of thing. He knew that Richard was one of those farmers making it pretty good out there on the farm all those years. Then just a couple years ago he turned the farm over to his boy, and then Richard and his wife moved into a nice house in the new addition of town. Wasn't long though and word got around town that Richard's wife had been acting peculiar out on the farm, wandering from their house in the middle of winter, wearing just her bathrobe and socks, all alone and talking nonsense. Eventually she didn't remember anything anymore, even poor Richard, they claimed. That was just the talk at the pool hall. Hell of a nice guy too, Russ thought, always real friendly and social and one who especially liked to joke around when he was playing cards. But for some reason Russ couldn't understand, the Frederiksens were never regular customers of Albrecht's Fairway—Russ knew who *did* and who *didn't* come through his doors, and the Frederiksens traded with him only for an occasional item or two. From his vantage point at the cash register, he could look out across the street and actually watch people going into the competitor, Super Valu. The Frederiksens, he would share with Lorraine, did the bulk of their shopping on Saturdays, always four or five big full bags. That, Russ would have to admit was his first thought now at the mention of Richard Frederiksen . . . those bags and bags of groceries hauled out of Super Valu over the years. Fact was, the more Russ would think about it now going forward, he didn't seem to have much, if anything, in common with the guy— after all, Richard wasn't a vet and didn't hunt or fish.

"Richard Frederiksen, you say?" Russ looked at the Pyrex dish again. "Well . . . why not? I'll see if he's down there. Anyway, I'll plan to see you here at my place about five-thirty. You remember the house, don't you? It's right next to Al Tillman's, the furnace man. You okay driving over?"

"Sure, sure, Russ, I get around pretty good in town. I remember your house too, the one with those Colorado evergreens in front, those evergreens you said you dug out in Estes Park years ago. You drove me past it when we came back from seeing that lawyer in Redwood about my accounts."

"That's right, the two evergreens. Well, good. Don't forget now, five-thirty."

"No, no, I'll be there! And, ah . . . thanks. See you later on then." The phone clicked.

Russ walked into the pool hall and right away spotted Richard Frederiksen at a table in the front. It was the usual bunch that played cards early in the afternoon, old Elmer Bendixen and one of his boys who stayed with him there on the farmstead, another farmer, Donnie Koblin, a bachelor who lived with his mother, and Rich. The lunch crowd had thinned, and Shelly was busy scraping the grill. "Hi, Russ!" she waved with her cleaning brush. I'll be with you in just a minute."

"Well, no hurry, Shelly, but you can bring me a cup of coffee over here—I'm going to check out this Sheepshead game." He couldn't just barge right into a conversation with Rich, there in front of everyone else, so he decided to bide his time, have his coffee and watch awhile. Rich was having fun with a practical joke, hiding a card after the deal so that the others were double-checking their hands, looking around their chairs, for the missing card. Russ couldn't help but laugh. He pulled up a chair behind Rich. "Don't' mind me, fellas—just going to watch to see if everyone's honest here . . . I see you're missing a card from the widow . . ."

"Sure, sure, Russ . . . we're on our last hand here. But darn if old Richard isn't slipping something by us again . . ." Elmer diverted his eyes only long enough to acknowledge Russ and then was back to tracking down the missing card. "Ah hah, ah hah! There it is . . . right there in his shirt pocket, right there in plain sight!" He flung his accusing finger out over the table at Rich. Rich put on an impish look as he plucked the card out of his pocket with the flair of a magician, and the others hooted as they shook their heads and rolled their eyes. "See there, Russel? This guy here, sweet old Richard Frederiksen, is always up to tricks . . . he's got to entertain, that's all there's to it . . . never seen anything like it . . . must be the Dane in him . . ." Elmer counted the cards in his hand again just for good measure and then leaned back in his chair. "Okay, boys, let's get this game finished . . . no need to re-deal, we'll just all know that there's a jack of diamonds in the widow this round . . ."

When the game finally ended and the guys started clearing out, Russ followed Rich out to his car. "Say, Richard, I was talking to Roy Hanson, and he claims that you—being a good sport and all—might take a notion to try out a *hotdish* just for the fun of it . . ."

Rich still had a twinkle in his eye, enjoying this additional banter after the card game and amused with the particular disdain Russ used with the word 'hotdish.' "A *hotdish*, you say," Rich tried to imitate Russ. "Well, I'm game for anything if it means a meal. What exactly "are you getting at, Russ?"

"Well, a daughter gave me this *hotdish* that I've had in the freezer now for a couple months, and I decided it better get used up. But it's a heck of a lot of food—what's a single fella going to do with it all? I invited Roy to help me out with it. Thought for sure he could use a meal and wouldn't complain much, being a bachelor and all. How about it—do you want to stop over for supper too? You know, about five-thirty? I don't know much about your likes and dislikes, but you're sure as heck welcome to join us."

"Well, I'm not soo sure, Russel . . ." Rich folded his arms and stood there with his head cocked as if contemplating—"I still have part of my scrumptious Meals on Wheels that I was planning on finishing up tonight. Hmmm, well . . ." The corners of his mouth were twitching into a smile. ". . . Okay then . . . I think I'll have to put that aside until tomorrow and see what sort of *hotdish* you have there, Russ!" His teeth flashed, and he winked.

"Well, good then! With three of us, we might be able to do some damage to it. Oh, and say, I should tell you where I live—across town from you, the street with Welter's Cabinets, you know, the old roller rink—my house is just down a couple blocks on the west side. I got two big evergreens in the front yard, the only evergreens on the block."

"Yes, sir, I know the street . . . and I'll give Roy a call . . . he can ride with me."

Rather than the deskwork he had planned for that afternoon, Russ found himself tidying up the house a bit, picking up here and there and giving the bathroom a once-over with his trusty jug of bleach. He figured it would be the kitchen or the bathroom with all the action. Lorraine's pill bottles were still all lined up on the kitchen counter like a collection of mementos for terminal illness. He brushed them into the waste basket with one sweep of his hand. All the while he whistled a quiet steady tune of Glen Miller's "Chattanooga Choo Choo," which had been on WCCO's "oldie" show that morning.

And now considering that the featured dish might require backup for the appetites of old farmers, just a little something to round out the meal, he rummaged for last-minute additions: a couple of his prize-worthy tomatoes ripened to perfection on the window sill as if waiting for this occasion to be showcased, a can of his favored peaches tucked back in the cupboard, half a loaf of Tastee bread, and, of course, coffee. "That should do it," he beamed as he wiped his hands after adding the last slice of tomato to the crystal plate which Lorraine always used to serve the summer feature. He peeked under the foil of the Pyrex dish in the oven, which now to his utter amazement, had been transformed into a gourmet delight, steaming and oozing smells of a midwest kitchen. "Fit for a king! Or, kings, should I say!" He closed the oven door, resumed "Chattanooga," and grabbed three low-balls from the cupboard.

The Chevy Caprice lurched into Russ's driveway a couple minutes before five-thirty—"well, I'll be darned, right on the button," Russ smiled as he glanced at the kitchen clock and watched from the window as the two old guys got out of the car, then stood there hitching up their pants and adjusting their glasses as they glanced around their surroundings to be sure they were at the correct address, obvious newcomers to the Albrecht house. As they shuffled to the door, one with a limp, Russ couldn't help but wonder what Lorraine would say right about now with his odd choice of companions, far-removed from their circle of friends, with nothing much in common really. "Who?" she might ask... "You invited who?" He felt a rush of independence as he quickly finished assembling a plate of olives, radishes and saltine crackers and went to the door.

"Well, come on in, fellas. You're right on time!"

Russ escorted the men to his kitchen table, eager now to offer his added surprise. He reached into the cupboard with a flourish and, like a porter at a five-star restaurant, presented a bottle of brandy. "How about a snort of this for happy hour, gentlemen? Only the finest here . . . Mr. Boston's Apricot Brandy—this stuff I learned about from old Otto Hanson years ago. We've got plenty of time, and this *hotdish* isn't going anywhere!" Not waiting for an answer, he began pouring.

"'Happy hour' . . . I always liked that name . . . . something we all could use, Russel. And that brandy suites me fine, yes, sir." Rich stood tall, poised with his head back sniffing in the smells from the oven. "Smells real good in here, Russel."

Roy sniffed too, nodding in agreement with a grin ready to burst. "And a real nice place you have here, Russel." He poked his head around the kitchen and out into the dining room and the TV room beyond.

"Say, and look here . . ." Rich was pointing to the plate of relishes in the middle of the table. "*Horses over* too! Russ here really knows how to entertain! This is a real banquet!"

The other two looked at each other with squinted eyes as they mouthed the words . . . '*horses over?*'

"Oh, come on, you two—like in the fancy menus—probably French or something. You know, *hors d'oeuvre*—but it always looks to me like . . . '*horses over!*'

"Oh, yeah . . . you're right . . . .sure . . . see what you mean . . . '*horses over*' . . . yeah . . ." Russ and Roy couldn't vow to any spelling but they laughed anyway. Russ finished pouring the brandy.

"There. Now, you take one of these glasses here, grab a chair, and help yourself to some of these . . . '*horses over.*' No hurry. Like I said, that hotdish isn't going anywhere!" Russ turned the oven dial down and pulled out a chair himself. "Now, Richard— I know a little bit about Roy here, but, maybe you can tell me how long it's been since you moved into town from the farm, you know, something about yourself . . ."

Russ in his kitchen flouring walleye.

Little did they know then, as they sipped their brandies at Russ's kitchen table that night, letting the smooth sweet liquor sit on their tongues, talking about farms and crops and weather and families, that the three had launched into what would be a most unusual chapter in their lives.

CHAPTER 8
COMRADES

He whispered, "Say, Albrecht, this is like a banquet, don't you think? Look at these fine rations . . . not to mention a roof over our heads!" It was Red Degenhardt with a wide smile, finding a space next to Russ on the dirt basement floor, using his helmet as a stool. Clarence Dale was on the other side of Russ, already busy eating from the small carton labeled just "chicken." He looked up as he chewed a big mouthful and motioned for Red to sit down. The large room was dim, lit only by a small candle in a tin can, centered on a block of wood retrieved from a stack of junk off to the side. The room's one high window was draped shut with a tarp so not even a speck of light could escape and give away this secret gathering of forty U.S. soldiers below, eating their rations in near silence. The First Battalion had taken the town that day and all was secure . . . but the enemy was just to the east. This was another one of those "unusual chapters" in Russ' life, but some forty-two years before his "banquet" with Roy and Richard. This time he ate with Red and Clarence, again glad for the company.

It was late November 1944 and the Thirtieth Division, 120th Infantry Regiment was "driving deep into the unknown fortress of

Germany on the heels of success," as field manuals tell the story. On November 16th, they had launched what was destined to make tactical military history as "the perfect infantry attack." Intense coordination with weeks of planning, preparation, patrolling, training and reconnaissance was the key to this surprise attack on the town of Euchen, Germany, a Secret Service stronghold. Without the usual cover of woods or night, the infantry troops defied all odds by advancing across an open 900 yards of ground in the middle of the day under a screen of artillery fire. They took the town by total surprise in just a matter of hours. In the following days the 120th Regiment made similar rapid advances and seized the towns of Linden and Neusen, again with minimal casualties (History of the 120th Infantry Regiment, *Washington Infantry Journal Press*).

Still, this war in Germany was foreboding to the allied troops, having enjoyed victory in France but knowing full well that the enemy was digging its heels in and preparing its defenses in a final desperate stand. The weather too added to the miseries of this war. Rain, mud, and near-freezing temperatures cast an ever-increasing gloom on the soldiers, even causing a rift between the infantry—like Red and Clarence and Russ—and the tankers. The rift it turned out was really the infantry's gripe—after all, it was the infantry leading the advances, sloshing and slipping through the muddy beet fields and catching any rest they could in mired foxholes, while the tankers followed as mobile artillery and found shelter in basements. "Why don't the tanks lead?" was the complaint by the infantry. "We can mop up, after the tanks go through, like we were taught in basic training!" The rationale seemed sound as the infantry grumbled over their conditions.

Before long, the infantry's complaints filtered to the top, and the officers and tank commanders met. "Okay," the tank commander reported, "we've got five light tanks for Company A. We're not going to go ahead of you and not behind you—we'll go right along with you . . . but we'll need four infantrymen to ride on top of each tank. As we go through towns, it will be the duty of you men riding on top to run up ahead to check crossroads for any enemy artillery, then to notify our gunner. If the crossroad is clear, you can wave the tank through." Such was the plan for the next advance. Private First Class Russel Albrecht, Staff Sergeant Hollis (Red) Degenhardt, and Private Clarence Dale were among the twenty infantrymen assigned to ride. Just lucky, they thought.

It was under these circumstances that Russ, Red, and Clarence now enjoyed the comforts of this cellar, dark and smelly, but a solid structure just the same, impenetrable to bullets it seemed and out of the rain. "Yeah, Red," Russ whispered back, "these ten-in-one rations with these tankers sure beat the old C-rations all to hell—look at the variety here, and none of that damned hash! You bet it's a banquet! Tankers don't know how nice they've got it." Clarence nodded in agreement as he chomped down on another spoonful of chicken.

The three fell into silence with the rest of the group then, infantry and tankers all together under a roof. They communicated only with nudges and gestures as they savored each bite, as if a last meal. Then, with the weariness of full stomachs and uneasy hearts, they settled into makeshift sleeping positions, now with their helmets as pillows, in the cramped quarters. The infantrymen, now in this luxury accommodation, nodded off in a more restful sleep than they'd known for the past two weeks.

The three had only become acquainted earlier in the month when the First Battalion was relieved for a two-day rest at a monastery near Kerkrade. There, not only were they free from the battles and constant vigil of the front, but they were free from rigid orders—they could relax. They slept in beds, ate seconds and thirds if they wanted, and were entertained at every meal by the Thirtieth Division orchestra. It was a haven. The soldiers played cards, wrote letters back home, and they talked.

Russ immediately took a liking to Clarence. "He's a heck of a good kid even though he's only a couple years out of high school," Russ wrote to Lorraine, " . . . he's from Ohio, and likes to fish and hunt, so we have that in common." Russ at age thirty-four with a wife and two small girls was almost a father-figure to Clarence, but then, in war, age can be irrelevant when soldiers share their sweet memories of back home, far from battlefields.

Then Red, a staff sergeant from Louisiana, had a flair for hitting it off with the troops. ". . . Just a regular guy," Russ wrote, "almost like one of us privates," and that's what Russ liked about him. Red laughed easily and took to Russ' storytelling, and when the conversations turned to a more serious side, Red liked to talk about his wife and their plans to start a family when he got home.

Morning in that cellar came with a tap on the shoulder in the dark and a whisper, "Up soldier, 500 hours." In silence, they ate the remaining rations, downed cold coffee, packed their gear and drew long breaths on a final cigarette before another day's advance. As Russ put out his Lucky, and as a matter of ritual, he checked his shirt pocket for the two carefully folded pages of coloring by his small daughters, carried with him since he was shipped out nine months ago, always there close to his heart. Those folded pages had been carried from the beaches of Normandy, northern France, Belgium, Holland, and now Germany. He headed up the stairs.

Russ resumed his position at the right rear of the third tank, the commander's tank. Red was in front, Clarence to his left, and a young kid from New York on the other front side. The Thirtieth Division's First Battalion was off to its next objective, the town of Erberich. The five light tanks rumbled along, staying even with the infantry, just as ordered. Noisy and awkward bulks of metal, the tanks lumbered, capable in their pure mass to maneuver the muddy fields and mow down the hedges and barbed-wire entanglements, all the while on the lookout to blow up a distant enemy if called upon. But the tanks were easy targets and nothing to compare with the German version, the Tiger Royal with its 88-mm gun—over twice the fire power of these light U.S. tanks.

The day was dreary again and quiet, the troops plodding eastward, the clanking, grinding tanks the only sound over sloshing boots. Hours passed. Then, out of nowhere almost and as if a celestial warning, fireballs shot across the sky, followed with explosions out of sight somewhere behind them. The tanks stopped. The hatch of the third tank opened, and like a periscope, the commander popped up with field glasses, assessing the situation 360 degrees.

"Sir, what happens if we meet a Tiger Royal up in the next town?" Russ didn't hesitate addressing the commander.

"Don't worry, Albrecht," he snapped, "if we see one, we're going to turn around and get the hell out of there." The commander disappeared and the hatch closed. They started up again.

Another pair of field glasses was eyeing the situation too, just ahead across the clearing. There, a Tiger Royal was nestled down on a sunken road with its 88-mm muzzle poked out of the hedge, sighting in the five light tanks. The tanks lumbered closer . . . closer . . . closer. *Whoom!* The first tank blew! *Whoom!* The second tank! And just as Russ was ready to jump—*whoom!* The third tank was hit! Within seconds, the last two tanks turned to retreat.

Bodies flew. In that instant, as Russ was hurled through the air, he saw Clarence hurling through the air too but it was as if in slow motion, with part of his neck and shoulder missing, and blood spraying like the metal pieces bursting from the tank. Red, in his position at the front of the tank disappeared like vapor. The moment of impact on that quiet French countryside was as though the earth erupted. The searing, breaking metal . . . the screams . . . were deafening. And then silence.

Russ opened his eyes to see only the thick clouds overhead. He questioned for a split second whether they were in fact heavenly, but then sensed reality with the over-whelming stench of burning parts. Squishy mud cradled his limbs. Stunned, Russ lay there wondering if he too had lost part of his body. He shook his head clear. By instinct he first grabbed his rifle, then picked himself up and scrambled for safety behind the battered tank. "Albrecht! Albrecht! Holy shit, everyone's dead but us!" The kid from New York crawled up next to Russ, his hands quivering as he stared out and positioned his rifle in the direction of the hedge. "We're out here alone! Holy shit!" His eyes were those of the frightened boy he was.

Alone now in that field with only the disabled tank as a shield, Russ knew they were sitting ducks. His eyes darted for options.

The Tiger Royal had yet another move to finish off the third tank—a phosphor shell. *Whoosh!* The shell hit in the front end and came out the back, thrusting a chunk of shrapnel deep into Russ's hip. "Awhhhh!" Even before the fiery pain registered, Russ sensed a dreamlike detachment from his body as if looking at someone else, a fascination really, seeing the odd four inches of metal sticking out from his hip, firmly lodged through his jacket and cartridge belt.

"You're hit!"

Russ looked back at the frightened eyes. "God damn it! We've got to get out of here—this thing is going to blow!" He motioned to the right with his rifle. "See that kraut hole over there? Let's make a run for it—I'll follow you, with this damned leg of mine."

"You sure you can make it?"

"It's a damn sight better than staying here—go, *go!*"

They dove into the hole just as the tank blew. Fragments of metal and bodies clouded the air as the flames swallowed up from deep inside the tank. Russ and the kid ducked as low as they could get in the shallow hole, holding their helmets close down over their eyes. They peeked out just over the hole's edge for their next move back to safe territory. The barbed-wire entanglements they had just driven over with the tanks, had bounced up again.

"Remember that stone wall? You know, just before we got to that barbed wire? That's where we've got to head."

"Yeah, but, holy shit—how do we get around that barbed wire now? It's back up!"

"We run like hell and take a flying leap, that's how. That Tiger Royal is probably sighting us up again . . ."

"But what about your leg?"

"All I can do is try. Just stay low, and run like hell—now *go!*"

The kid took off with the speed of a sprinter out of the blocks, in spite of his heavy gear. He kicked up mud with each stride. Then, with the same athletic precision, he launched into a life-saving leap, clearing the entanglement with room to spare. Russ with the chunk of metal in his hip hobbled behind in a makeshift skip, but double-time. He heaved himself up and over—almost. Like dead weight, his wounded leg dropped into the entanglement where he now hung as an easy target in the snare of barbed wire.

Before he could get his breath, *whoosh!* The Tiger Royal fired again. The shell whirred by with the force of a straight-line wind, taking Russ's helmet with it. But, perhaps that shell was divine intervention quick to assist in what could be assumed a hopeless situation because it was that same force that propelled Russ over the entanglement to safety.

Behind the stone wall, a medic was attending to the injured. The remains of Red and Clarence lay out on that field.

CHAPTER 9
TWO MEN IN A KITCHEN

Yeah, hello—Rich?" Russ knocked on the screen door again, this time harder. He could hear Twins baseball blaring from a radio inside and could smell something frying. "RICH, you there?" He shaded his eyes up against the screen to look in.

"Oh, for Pete's sake, I wondered what all that racket was," Rich was hurrying to the door with a spatula in his hand and an apron around his waist, a pink and white embroidered apron similar to Lorraine's, Russ noticed. "Come on in, Russ, and make yourself comfortable! Gotta get back to the stove real quick so I don't ruin the meat. Just come on in!" He spun on his heels and hurried ahead of Russ through the hall back to the kitchen. "Wouldn't that look good on the menu . . . *a la charred* Swiss steak?" he laughed big and hearty, which jiggled his entire frame and made the apron seem even more comical. Russ felt at home.

"Sorry if you were standing there long, out there in this heat. My hearing isn't much good anymore so I don't mind if you YELL once in a while," he chuckled. "I see you have a hearing aid too, so we should get along just fine . . . say, what's that you have there?" He reached across the counter to turn down the volume on the radio.

Russ was so preoccupied with his new surroundings and Rich's exuberance that he forgot all about the bag in his arms. "Oh . . . these are tomatoes, a couple of cukes, and a head of broccoli I thought you could use. My darned garden is really putting out the stuff this year and, with Lorraine gone, I'm just not able to keep up with it. Now, I've got to tell you . . . I'm not much on cukes, never have been . . . but maybe you like 'em . . . Lorraine sure did. I'll set this stuff here on the table." He could see that every inch of the small countertop was already taken with an assembly line of ingredients. He took off his cap and hung it on the back of one of the kitchen chairs.

"Well, thank you, Russel! Thanks very much indeed. I've always heard you were quite the gardener." Rich bowed graciously with his spatula still in his hand. "Me, coming from the farm, you know, I could raise plenty of corn and soybeans, but never had time for the garden, so that was my wife's deal. I'll tell you what—we can use all this stuff for our meal tonight and do it up real good." He stood at the stove as he spoke, watching carefully to turn the floured meat patties at just the right moment. Traces of flour were scattered on the counter, the floor, and now on the side of his nose. Russ grabbed a sponge from the sink and began wiping up the counter.

"See? I just knew that you were good in the kitchen, too! I'll even give you an apron and you can get busy peeling those spuds there that I've set out." With one hand still flipping the patties, Rich reached in a drawer with his other for an apron, this one a gingham lime green, and he tossed it to Russ. "Isn't this great, Russel—maybe we'll become famous and start throwing dinner parties, the two of us!" and he laughed as he flipped a patty.

"Well, maybe so, Rich, but, this looks like a hell of a lot of food you got here for just you, me, and Roy." Russ looked at the potatoes piled high and the unopened packages of meat patties.

"Oh, I forgot to mention—I invited a couple more fellas, Elmer Bendixen and Hubert Iffert, friends of mine from the Farmers' Elevator Board. They lost their wives too a while back. Big eaters they are too, Russel—but I've got plenty here, and you and I can whip this up in no time." He scooped up the browned patties two at a time into a roaster and opened the second package. "You, of course, are acquainted with Elmer and Hubert—both been around a long time. Gosh, Elmer, he's almost ninety now, I think, and Hubert, he's about our age—you know, real young." He took his eyes off the stove just long enough to wink at Russ.

"Ha, young, you say." Russ shook his head. "But, yeah, I know those two—not real good of course with them being farmers, different churches too—in fact, that sounds about like you and me . . ." He snickered, knowing Rich might appreciate a little kidding.

"Isn't that so, Russel—and you even invited me for hotdish! Why I'll bet you're not even Danish!" Rich flipped a patty high and caught it with the pan. "But here we are cooking up a meal, the two of us!" With extra flair, he slapped each patty with the spatula, then turned to Russ with a mischievous grin and a look of concern. "You aren't Danish, are you?

"For heaven's sake, no!" Russ felt a rush of pleasure as he joined in Rich's game. "But I am proud to be half Norwegian . . ." He raised his eyebrows waiting for the comeback.

"Norwegian! Oh, no! They're the worst!" With a twisted scowl, Rich slapped his leg, and they both howled.

The clowning almost drowned out the organ music from the radio, signaling the end of the inning. Rich waved a time-out as he reached over to turn up the radio again. The announcer broke in, "Well, folks, it's the seventh inning stretch, here at Metropolitan Stadium here in beautiful Bloomington, Minnesota—Twins 5, Yankees 2." At that news, Rich yelped and began a little jig to the music right there at the stove.

"Okay! That's our Twins, yes, siree!" Russ tied his apron with a big grin. He knew that, Swiss steak or not, this was going to be a brand new kind of experience. "Yes, sir, sounds like we could win this one!"

For the next three-quarters of an hour, the two peeled and sliced, fried and boiled, buttered and mashed, salted and simmered. They peered over and under their bifocals, tending to the details of the meal with great ease, the way one might expect on an old men's version of the Julia Child show. The background Twins play-by-play triggered a rhythm and gusto to the details of the meal preparation lending an extra pat of this or dab of that with a timely slide or catch.

"What do you think, Russel? Needs a little more salt?" Rich held out a spoon of the tomato sauce from the roaster he had just pulled from the oven.

"Heck, don't ask me about salt—I'll always put more on. Can't taste like I used to." But Russ on cue took the spoon from his new cooking buddy and slurped just a smidgeon of the steaming tomato gravy. "Hmmm, that's darned good, Rich. Reminds me of the stewed tomatoes my mom used to put over fried eggs. Yeah, darned good."

"*Voila!*" Rich with the flair of a magician re-sealed the foil and pushed the roaster back into the oven. "Terrific! Now we can just sit down for a minute and wait for the boys to arrive. You like brandy, I know. How about you reach in that cupboard there for some glasses, and I'll mix up a couple of brandy-and-sevens, and we'll start happy hour early." Without waiting for an answer his head disappeared into the refrigerator as he searched for the Seven-Up. Russ still could hear him chuckling. "Good idea, Rich—we'll start early . . ."

As Rich prepared the drinks, Russ wandered just off the kitchen into the living room taking in the details of Rich's home, which though a much newer model than his, seemed very much like his own. The sameness that caught Russ's eye was in the woman's touch —a ceramic knick-knack collection, a bouquet of imitation flowers in a ribboned basket, flowered sofa pillows, a souvenir spoon display, a grouping of family photos in decorative frames—this home like his own looked stopped in another time. But one item stood out in contrast to the feminine orderliness: the recliner. With a slightly worn cushion, a rumpled pillow at the back and newspapers scattered alongside on the floor, the chair looked like a stubborn old friend. On the lamp table lay a remote control with the current issue of *T.V. Guide*. Just like his own.

"Say, Rich, do you watch that new show, *Oprah?*" He headed back into the kitchen.

Rich had two drinks ready and handed one to Russ. "Here, give this a try. In fact, let's toast! To, ah . . . to putting together a swell meal! How 'bout that?"

"I'll toast to that, darned right! And I'll just add—to many more!" Their glasses clinked, and the men downed big swallows of the refreshing drink. "Ahh," they both said at the same time, grinned about it, and then toasted again.

"Now, Russel, you were asking, about watching Oprah—you bet I watch her. How else is a guy going to keep up these days on all the important topics such as, oh, dating—bad husbands—diets, you name it!" Rich had raised both arms in a dramatic shrug and with a sly grin. "How about you? Do you watch her?"

"Yeah, I sure do. The show fits very nicely with my afternoon snooze time, if you know what I mean . . ." Russ tried to look serious. ". . . but the hell of it is sometimes I don't get to *snooze* when she gets going on some of those wild topics of hers. Hell, a lot of that stuff used to be off limits. You know, censored!" He broke out into a laugh. "Last week she had this woman talking about sex therapy—Ruth, I think here name was—funnier than hell."

"I saw that too, Russel! Wasn't she something?" Rich shook his head in amazement. "We'll have to keep watching—might learn something, huh?" He jabbed Russ on the arm and then turned back to the stove. "Oh, I'd better check the oven one more time. Don't want to ruin the meal just because we're busy talking about sex therapy, now do we? Ha!"

Still grinning, Russ took another long sip of his drink and then held the glass out to view it from all angles. "Say, Rich, this is a darned good drink, yes, sir." He smacked his lips in approval. "Brandy and Seven-Up, you say? Hmm, yes, sir—darned good." Standing in the kitchen hallway, he could see out the front screen door to the driveway where a big green Buick had coasted up. "Say, Rich, looks like your company is just about right on time."

Rich turned to look too. Three doors opened even before the car had come to a complete stop, and then a leg appeared from each green door. Russ chuckled to himself, reminded of the giant grasshopper he had encountered just that morning out near his cabbages. "Looks like they're hungry too by the way they're getting out so fast. Looks like they can't even wait for the car to stop."

"Sure enough. Those boys are never late for a meal!" Rich double-checked the clock, then set his drink down and hurried to the door. Russ took a big gulp and followed.

First out of the big Buick was Roy with his unassuming eagerness and smile, so familiar to Russ. He nearly tripped over his slow foot in his eagerness to get out of the car. Russ always got an instant boost just seeing Roy, always quick to smile even with his setbacks.

The other two fellows Russ knew, of course, with Morgan being such a small community. The truth was he just never needed to know *more* about them. Old Hubert Iffert and Elmer Bendixen were a couple more farmers who, to Russ's way of thinking, were sitting pretty darned good from their years on the farm. "Well-off and yet pinching every damned penny," was how Russ described them to Lorraine back when he ran the grocery store and saw first-hand their buying habits. "Oh, sure, they're the first in the door when it comes to coupon specials or loss-leaders or turkey drawings!" Other than that, Russ would notice them—in fact just like he noticed Rich—supporting the competitor across the street. He'd even overheard Dorothy at the pool hall say they were part of a group now who were buying groceries at the new Walmart in Redwood Falls, not even supporting the local merchants. Not veterans either, and not interested in the sorts of pastimes Russ enjoyed—hunting and fishing. Farmers, pretty well-set financially— that's what he knew for sure, and that was how he saw the two of them as they stepped out of the Buick. As for seeing a grasshopper in all this, well, that made him smile.

"Looks like 'boys night out,' doesn't it, Russ? Ah, I should say, *old* boys night out, the way they're fumbling around just getting out of the car, ha . . ." Rich was amused like a proud sibling. "Oh, Russ, hope you don't mind me asking them—got to stick together, us guys. Good old boys, that's what they are."

Russ looked again, even squinted as if that would reveal some of the virtues of the two men coming up the walk with his buddy

Roy. Surprisingly, cast in this new light—the category of old guys—he could see that they weren't much different from himself, really—guys who had lost their wives. "Well, I'll have to say, Rich, any of your friends are just fine with me."

Hubert was taller than the other two, and he carried his lanky frame like the stoic farmer he was. His face revealed a lifetime of conscientious farm work, a face that didn't smile much over the years so that now with age and ill-fitting dentures, it wore a frown. He was full-blood German and attended St. Michael's Catholic Church. Not too many years ago, Hubert and his wife moved from the farm into town to a handy location just across the street from the church. Hubert turned the farmstead over to his son Arnie, who attended to the farm in the meticulous manner of his father. And being the good son he was, Arnie invited old Hubert to participate in the planting and harvesting each year. That's when Hubert came closest to a true smile, back on his farmstead. There at the edge of Morgan, all fenced in crisp white, the farm was picture-perfect—just ideal, Russ always thought as he drove by. Yet still more of the original farmstead extended across the highway, and it was those acres that Hubert sold for quite a decent price to the nursing home back in the fifties. Now, the fact that the nursing home sat on his land was a topic of great pride for old Hubert. And, after that move into town, he and his wife even set off to new ventures, traveling much of the year to far away places like Europe. "The most traveled man in Morgan"—that's what the front page story in *The Morgan Messenger* said a few years back. Russ wondered about that now because from what he had overheard in the pool hall, now that Hubert's wife was gone, he pretty much stayed closed up in his house most days and only drove his car once a week to size-up the neighboring farm fields.

Elmer, on the other hand, smiled easily—he seemed to have a trick up his sleeve. He was heavy-set and solid, usually with that sly smile. Russ got the impression that Elmer was as much a serious businessman as a hard-working farmer when Elmer took to discussing the stock market at the card table. The stock market wasn't exactly a big topic for most of the Morgan residents more suited to consider the effect of compound interest in their savings account. But for someone like old Elmer with what appeared to be adequate financial wherewithal, the ups and downs of the NYSE was a topic he enjoyed. The Bendixen family had one of the largest farms in the area, and, with Elmer up in years, his two boys did most of the farming. The single son lived with Elmer after Elmer's wife died, and the married one lived in a second house there on the Bendixen farmstead. Elmer attended the little Danish Lutheran Church out in the country just a few miles west of Morgan. Russ figured Elmer had to be close to ninety years old, but still looked spry with just a slight limp as he came up to the front door.

"Well, if this isn't a sight for sore eyes!" Rich beamed as he held open the screen door. "Watch that step now so we don't have to run to the hospital before dinner," he laughed. "Elmer, don't go thinking you're a spring chicken just because you've got those new knees!"

"Yeah, yeah, I'm a spring chicken and don't you forget it!" Elmer formed a roguish grin, and his eyes twinkled like Santa as he stepped inside, all the while sizing up Russ. "Well, look here . . . it's Russel Albrecht. Hello there, Russel!"

"Hello, hello!"

Elmer nabbed Russ on the shoulder. "You're looking slim and full of energy. Why you're just a kid here like Hubert, I'm sure of that." He nudged Hubert who was behind him.

Hubert grunted and responded like the straight man in a stand-up comedy. "Yeah, I'm the kid—seven years behind you, Elmer. You're the spring chicken, and I'm the kid." When he spoke, his angular jaw seemed to be hinged like a puppet and his teeth clattered. His mouth still wore the frown, but his eyebrows lifted, revealing a slight twinkle in his soft, pale-blue eyes, as he looked down at Elmer. He gave a nod to Russ and Roy and stepped inside.

Roy, content to observe, just nodded and smiled, following at the heels of the other two. "Hi, fellas!" He tipped his cap. "How about those Twins? They're winning, you know. We were listening to them in the car!"

"Yes, the Twins! We've been listening too here in the kitchen.

Come in, come in. Make yourselves at home, and I'll serve up some brandy sevens. Russel here and I have been cooking up quite a storm!"

"Hmm, something smells mighty good." Elmer led the way through the hall, following the aromas. Then adding from the corner of his mouth, "And if those aprons mean anything, we're in for a treat, hee, hee."

The five finally settled down for the spread, but not before Rich and Russ made a wild dash to ready the table, in more or less a vaudeville routine, with the smooth brandy sevens having long-settled their nerves. They darted about finding plates and utensils, pulling in extra chairs, tearing off paper towels for napkins. The other three watched in wonder as they clutched their drinks and waited for the high-sign to sit down.

"Okay, boys, have a seat—dinner is served!" Rich announced as he set a steaming platter and bowl in the middle of the table. "This is a favorite of mine—Swiss steak and mashed potatoes. But really, I should call it 'Swiss steak with a little Dane in it,' now shouldn't I?" He put his finger to his chin and smiled.

"Swiss, Danish—whatever the name, I say it looks darned good. None of us are going to be complaining." Russ eyed the others who were already reaching for the food.

"And boys, I want you to know that Russ brought us some broccoli and cucumbers fresh from his garden. Oh, and perfect tomatoes!" He wheeled around for the plate, but Russ was already holding it out to display the heap of bright red tomato slices.

"Hey, isn't there a song about tomatoes? You know, it's a cowboy-kind-of-song, heard it just last week on 'CCO. How does it go . . . hmm, la, la . . . two things . . . la, la . . . that's it, I've got it . . . 'only two things that money can't buy, that's true love and homegrown tomatoes!' . . . da, da!" Rich bowed to the plate of tomatoes with his final notes.

"Don't know anything about that tune, but can't argue with

it." Russ set the plate down and took his place at the table, pleased. Rich settled in his chair too, still humming, and then the table turned quiet, just that fast, with only the sounds of eating, a fan whirring from the counter, and play-by-play baseball.

As Elmer scraped the last bite of potatoes from his plate, he eased back in his chair with his hands folded across his belly. "Delicious, Richard, and you too, Russel—I know you were a team with this meal. Yes, sir, this was mighty good. You two must have taken lessons from your wives, I can tell. Heh, heh, maybe it's the aprons . . ."

"Yeah," Hubert, suddenly vocal, broke in, "this beats Meals-on-Wheels any day. Humph."

"That goes for me, too!" Roy grabbed one more sliced tomato and busied himself with the salt and pepper.

"Well, I've got to say, Rich here introduced me to something new—this Swiss steak, or whatever you call it. Never had that before, I can tell you. I'm a little picky with these choppers of mine, but had no trouble, and it was darned good!" Russ took one last swallow of coffee.

Rich acknowledged the compliment with his gracious smile, leaning back in his chair to soak it all in. "Couldn't have done it without Russ's help, but you know, it worked out pretty good . . . ah, huh . . . pretty good . . ." Then with a start, his eyes opened wide as he tilted his head to the radio. He jumped up, waving to signal everyone quiet. He cranked up the volume just as the announcer gave the count in the ninth inning: "Three balls, two strikes. It's a pitch . . . he's OUT! Twins win, 5 to 4!"

The five cheered and raised their glasses.

CHAPTER 10
THE GANG

The red Ford Taurus, dusty from the rural gravel roads, turned out from the Texaco station burped full. Russ's six-seater headed down Third Street on its route, so familiar with trips once or twice a week these last ten months, as if it were on a track.

Just two houses before the T in the road, where the ominous Catholic Church sat, the Taurus turned left into Hubert Iffert's driveway, neat and tidy. The lawn was edged in precision form, with a brick pathway leading to the back door of the crisp white rambler. Hubert's angular face was framed in the window, watching for his ride. In a matter of a minute or two, the Taurus backed out of the driveway, turned at the T and headed to Vernon Avenue, the main street of town, only a couple of blocks away.

On Vernon Avenue, the Taurus pulled up alongside Donnie Koblin's tan Ford Bronco, easy to spot parked alone in front of the Farmland Harvester store now closed for the day. All of the other cars on Morgan's only downtown street were clustered in front of the VFW for a busy Friday night with the Oscarson wedding reception and dance scheduled at eight o'clock, with a special performance by Ollie Larson on the concertina. Donnie was waiting at his designated pick-up place. This stop was new for the Taurus, just since a month ago when Donnie's mother, old Mrs. Koblin finally died and Donnie found himself all alone out there on the farm with no good cooking skills and a heart condition and episodes of depression to boot. He happened to be Elmer's baseball buddy, and lucky for him, Elmer took note of Donnie's stark life and invited him into the group. Since the Koblin farm was out of the way really, north of town about five miles and since Donnie was probably twenty years younger than the rest and could easily drive the five miles into town, the designated pick-up seemed only appropriate. He was happy to be included.

The Taurus started out again and turned left off Vernon Avenue at Highway 67, Morgan's only intersection with a stoplight, a precaution thought necessary by the city council a few years ago because of the increased activity with the expanding grain elevators on that stretch of road. On Highway 67, the Taurus headed east four blocks to the edge of town where it turned onto Second Street and stopped in front of Roy Hanson's one-bedroom house, that tiny house which stood out for its smallness, even among the modest framed homes on that edge of town. Roy was sitting on the front step ready to go, humming a jingle as he tapped his good foot.

Back the way it came on Highway 67, the Taurus turned to the new addition just south off the highway. These homes were new and bigger, some even with decks and attached garages, and yards flanked by cornfields there on the edge of town. The Taurus coasted into Richard Frederiksen's driveway, greeted by a colorful *"Velkommen"* sign in scrolled red-and-blue lettering, the kind found in Scandinavian gift shops in the Twin Cities, displayed with a certain prominence at the side of the door. Richard was standing out on the lawn talking with his neighbor Wilbur Best, and Richard waved a wide hello as the Taurus drove up. In only a few months, the car would have an empty seat and Wilbur in fact would be part of this pick-up route, but not today.

The Taurus had just one more stop, out in the country, southwest on County Road 68 which led to Sanborn Corners and then on to Redwood Falls. After three miles, the Taurus turned right at the Elmer Bendixen mailbox and made its way down the quarter-mile driveway to the grand, white farmhouse.

"Dad, I can hear them coming. Are you set to go? Your *Vroom* driver is here!" Norman chuckled as he looked out the window as the dusty red Taurus lurched to a stop exactly in line with the sidewalk, exactly as it did each time it stopped to pick up Elmer.

"Yeah, yeah. See you later." Elmer adjusted his cap with a quick snap and lumbered out the door and down the sidewalk to the car.

The Taurus, full now with all six of the old men, sped out the quarter-mile driveway, whipping up a cloud of dust behind so that when it stopped sharply at the highway, the dust cloud quickly caught up with the Taurus for just a few seconds, hovered, then drifted away with the spring breeze.

"Okay, fellas, which way? Where is it going to be tonight?"

Half drill sergeant and half tour guide, Russ shifted into "park" and sat with his fingers drumming the steering wheel, motor running, waiting for a decision.

"We've been to New Ulm quite a few times this spring."

"Last week it was Klostner . . ."

"My meal last time at Springfield wasn't that good, but maybe it was just a one time deal—actually, now that I think of it, might have been just the powdered potatoes, I didn't like."

"Sleepy Eye doesn't have anything on a Friday night . . . closed up tighter than a drum. What about that new place in Fairfax, there by the big gas station, 'Highwy 4 Eats' . . . some name like that?"

"Naw, that's not supposed to open for another week."

"Mr. Steak in New Ulm always has that good salad bar. I don't care how many times we've been there."

"But we're going there next week for Hubert's birthday, remember?"

"Oh, yah . . . Hubert, you buying?" Chuckles.

"Humph . . . "

"There's always Country Kitchen in Redwood—I like that most of the time. Just don't order the fish sandwich."

"I'm pretty new to this—I'll take anything."

"Say, what about the Food Shed in Redwood? They've got that buffet which isn't too bad, all you can eat . . . We're pretty hungry tonight, aren't we?"

"I am."

"Me too—okay by me."

"Yup, that's fine."

"Me, too. What about you, Russ?"

"The Food Shed? Yup, that's okay with me . . . Redwood it is!" Russ shifted out of park with the flair of a New York cabbie and turned right onto the highway heading west, just as the sun was setting behind a bower of trees on the horizon.

The drive would be another fifteen miles which, by design, meant just enough daylight left to take in the wonder of the farmlands yet another time—a pastime these good Minnesotans never tired of. The countryside was as much a part of them as their own mother's home-cooking. On this drive, the new crops were just beginning to peak through the black, black dirt, forming straight rows of tender bright green, promises of a bountiful harvest in the short growing season of the upper Midwest, which is the miracle of it all after six months of frozen ground.

Planting, harvesting, the weather, the price of beans and corn, by-gone days of various farm families, the abandoned farmsteads—that's what they talked about as they rode along through the lush farming country with fields as far as one could see in all directions, spotted only with groves of trees every half mile or so framing and sheltering the farm houses, barns and silos. Though not a farmer, Russ didn't hesitate to chime in on the conversation. He knew the subject from a vantage point they knew little about: For seventy years he had been the merchant whose livelihood depended upon the prosperity of the farming community—them. He liked to point that out. But sometimes, like this evening after a lonesome afternoon, he was content just to have company for a ride in the country and to share a meal.

As Russ listened to the others talk about hard times of the past, he couldn't help but wonder at how it peculiar that he was driving these well-to-do farmers. Where were they when his grocery business finally had to give in to the competition of the nearby towns? Likely, they were shopping in those nearby towns. And now, here they were, all thrown in together, like names drawn from a hat. That's what he was thinking as the car sped down the highway. He smiled to himself and shook his head in wonderment.

"So what're you smiling about there, Russel? What're you thinking?" Elmer had just given a serious dissertation on the crisis of big farming operations taking over the family farms—big operations like the gigantic barns they had just passed, high-tech barns housing thousands of turkeys. "Changing the face of agriculture forever," is what he'd read in the *Redwood Gazette*, and he added that these changes were already causing serious differences among the members at the Morgan Elevators Exchange. Turns out a couple of neighboring farmers north of town weren't even on speaking terms anymore.

"Smiling? Oh, yeah, guess I was thinking: well, that's life! One way or another, we have to fit in with the times. Refusing to talk to anyone, like those farmers you were telling about, Elmer . . . well, darn it, that's not going to get you anywhere."

Just as Russ finished, they had passed the city limits sign for Redwood Falls, so the issue of the farming operations was put on hold as the car slowed down, and their attention turned to looking at the implement dealers at the edge of town, the new Walmart, and a residential neighborhood with a brand new high school. Just a couple of blocks after the town's main intersection, the Taurus took a sharp right into a small parking lot in front of a tacked-on sort of building, re-made from an A&W root beer stand, now with a marquee "The Food Shed." Russ cranked the steering wheel, turning into the last available parking space near the front door, coming to an abrupt stop at the curb. Everyone lurched forward and then back. "There you are, boys. How's that for a good spot!" He was pleased. "Now I don't want to hear any bellyaching about how far you had to walk. Sure looks like this place is busy tonight, too, so let's get the heck in there and get a table!"

They piled out of the car a limb at a time, a gangly group with feed elevator caps, bodies hunched. The air smelled of fried food and cigarette smoke venting from the building mixed with fresh fertilizer from the field of corn just a block north.

"Welcome, gentlemen! What do we have, a party of six? Do you have a reservation?" It was a new waitress meeting them at the door. She looked like she was fresh out of high school, with menus and notebook in hand like text books.

"Yeah, six of us . . ." Russ always took the lead with details, plus he was the fastest walker, so he was always in front. But Rich, seizing yet another opportunity to have some fun, leaned ahead of Russ and interrupted in a high-nose, city-like voice, "Yes, six of us . . . we're here with the, ah . . . Grabowskis, yes, the Graboswki party, Richard Grabowski." He straightened himself a little taller. Russ raised his eyebrows in surprise, but then knew enough to keep quiet. He adjusted his cap to avoid eye contact with the waitress and ducked back.

"Grab-ow-ski, you say?

"Ah, huh."

"Yes, let me check." Her worried eyes glanced down the list of names in her notebook, twice. "Hmmm, I don't see that name. I'll go in the back room and check for you. Just wait here please." She smiled a quick half smile and left them standing there as she walked to the back room, flipping back through her list, and talking to herself.

"Richard! That's the same trick you played at Mr. Steak in New Ulm! Pretty soon they're going to be on the lookout for our bunch!" Roy had to stifle his laugh into his hand and crouched back in with the others. They glanced at each other, like school boys caught in a prank, their shoulders quivering with their pent-up amusement.

"Shhh, here she comes." Rich tried to look concerned.

"I'm so sorry, gentlemen, but we just don't have a Grobowsky party tonight. Did you call today?"

By then the guys couldn't contain themselves any longer and burst into giggles, but with their heads down, a little ashamed when they saw her innocent, perplexed expression.

"No, no, we didn't call at all. Just a joke . . . just a joke . . . no Grabowskis and no reservation . . . sorry, miss," Rich wished now he had played the joke on maybe one of the older waitresses. Still it was fun to get all the guys to laugh, and he couldn't help but look amused. "We were just having a little fun tonight—just us bunch of old fellas getting out, you know. Isn't that a terrible joke?" Her eyes were nodding yes, but Rich hurried on before she had time to reconsider. "But, miss, if you would happen to have a table for us, we'd surely appreciate it and wouldn't be much trouble . . ." Comic and trick-player, Rich still was always a gentleman. His eyes sparkled.

She looked up at him with a pained expression and then broke out in a laugh herself, relieved that she hadn't made a mistake on this, only her second night on the job. "You had me there and I should have known better with those silly grins on your faces . . . Ah, and yes . . . I do just happen to have a table for you—it's being cleared right now. Just follow me."

"Oh, that's mighty nice of you, miss." Rich turned and winked at the five men lined up behind him. "Come on, boys. This fine lady has a table for us."

As she led the group to the back room, Elsie, one of the veteran waitresses who was bringing a tray of food out of the kitchen to another table, smiled and shook her head as she noticed the six old men filing in. "Carrie, don't let those guys play any tricks on you. I should have warned you about them . . ."

A buffet suited them just fine with ample choices and with just one price—simple. The chalkboard shouted: "$5.95 BUFFET—ALL YOU CAN EAT, BUT EAT WHAT YOU TAKE!" The salad bar which was touted as the best in Redwood County included not only the usual salad fixings but the owner's special recipes for pickled pigs feet and venison salami, along with the new imitation crab meat just out on the market, plus two jello varieties, and a chocolate pudding. And, coffee. They dug in, oblivious to anything other than the plates in front of them, with the restaurant din a tranquilizing background tune.

Russ passed on the chocolate pudding dessert and was content to savor his last bite of mashed potatoes followed by a swallow of coffee. He pushed his chair back to wait for the others. "Holy smokes, Elmer, you just now starting on seconds?" He pretended to look surprised, waiting for the usual comeback.

Elmer returning to his chair again, glanced at Russ's empty plate and then his own, full to the edge with mashed potatoes and gravy, a slab of roast beef, a chicken leg, and a scoop of red Jell-O, wobbling and oozing into the brown gravy. "Well, Russel . . . I just don't know how you pack in so much so quick. I saw you getting seconds. Maybe I just jabber too much. And you don't have any fat on you either! I can't figure that out." He chuckled to himself and shook his head as he picked up his fork and knife again and began to cut up the beef, accustomed now to Russ's impatience. "Yeah, you're a *vroom* driver and a *vroom* eater, that's for sure." He dove into his plate again, unconcerned.

Russ chuckled. This was their routine. The other four were still busy finishing their meals too, but it was Elmer that Russ liked to pick on, the elder of the group, who just happened to love to eat. And at age ninety-one, if a guy loved to eat, could still get around and have a good time, well, more power to him. That was how Russ saw it. "Yeah, yeah, Elmer, you just take your time. I'm going to get another refill on coffee . . . that is, if I can get our waitress back here . . . heck, where is she anyway . . ."

He sat up tall and looked around the room, his fingers tapping on the table as usual. The place was bustling with activity, chatter, dishes clanging. "There she is." He did a little wave, but she disappeared behind the swinging doors. "Gosh darn it!" He turned back in his chair, and that's when it happened. At that precise moment, before Russ had completely turned around so that his view of the table was diagonal, that's when dental fixatives suddenly became an issue. That's when Hubert, from across the table, sneezed. Now this wasn't an ordinary sneeze, even as sneezes go from crusty, old, rough-around-the-edges men, but it was the no-holds-barred kind of sneeze with such force and such a gush of air, and without any warning whatsoever, that anyone nearby would normally be concerned and be prompted to say, "Are you all right?" But no one did. Elmer, Rich, Roy, and Donnie just kept on eating with their heads to their plates. Russ, on the other hand, was busy watching Hubert's *teeth*, the bottom plate, that is . . . *fly* across the table! The pink dentures barely missed the napkin holder, passing to Russ's left, directly between Richard and Donnie, who were sitting just across from Hubert. An aimed shot couldn't have been better. Russ, still half-turned in his chair, froze for a second to register what just went on, shifting his eyes ever so slightly to see that the other guys were preoccupied with their eating, and that he, apparently, was the only witness. "*Well* . . ." he bit his lip, ". . . I wonder if she'll ever come around with more coffee . . ." Thankful to have a task, he kept his neck craned toward the kitchen. His fingers speeded up the tapping.

"*Gesundheit!*" Rich, as if sedated from his full stomach and totally clueless that the odd pink-and-white projectile had just whizzed past his shoulder, casually looked up from his food in time only to see Hubert reaching in his pocket for his handkerchief. Hubert blew two loud snorts.

"Yeah, *gesundheit* . . . God bless you." Roy was preoccupied, wiping his bread across the last bit of gravy on his plate.

Well, perhaps this was the most peculiar incident that Russ had ever witnessed—at least, peculiar in terms of body malfunctions. Straight out of a comic strip, he thought. This was so out of line with normal order that his impulse was to throw back his head and laugh out loud with a hoop and holler. This was even funnier than when old Verna Klemp's hosiery suddenly rolled down while she was up at the communion rail a couple of years ago. He and Lorraine just about choked with amusement at the sight as they sat stoic in their pew. But this denture incident, like Verna Klemp's unfortunate hosiery, was another one of those compromised human predicaments where he knew for absolute certain that laughing out loud was *not* an option. He clenched his jaw instead to tamp down that urge. He kept his gaze out across the room and instinctively bit down hard on his tongue. Mercifully, just at that moment the waitress re-appeared from the swinging doors, and Russ with the finesse of a used car salesman somehow channeled this surge of laughter which had been bubbling uncomfortably inside into a vigorous clearing of his throat, at the same time signaling her with his raised coffee cup. "There she is!" He cleared his throat again and swallowed hard. It hurt.

Meanwhile, as if this was just ordinary, everyday business to be tended to, Hubert, dead-pan and without a word, got up from his chair, ambled around to the other side of the table, picked up the teeth, brushed them off with a quick swipe on his pants, placed them back into that large downward-turned mouth, returned to his place at the table and resumed eating his chocolate pudding. The only evidence of the incident was the track of chocolate pudding droplets across the table.

Russ drank big swallows of the hot coffee now and held tight to the coffee cup, as he looked straight ahead at Elmer, his eyes steering clear of Hubert. He ran his tongue over his own false teeth assuring himself that they were tightly in place. He cleared his throat. "So Elmer . . . how are those two boys of yours getting along with the farm? They sure are heck of nice fellas." And he continued to bite down hard on his tongue.

Thankfully, for Russ—and for Hubert—the conversation about the Bendixen boys and then the related topic of disappearing old-time farm family arrangements continued until they all had finished their last bites and had leaned back in their chairs, content. Elmer put his napkin next to his plate, "Well, boys, are we set to go?"

Grateful for the set price of a buffet, the six didn't go through the usual knit-picking with the bill—they just had to divide, then throw in their usual few dimes and nickels for a tip. They shuffled out of the Food Shed back into the night air. Elsie waved goodbye, "See you next week, gentlemen." She stopped clearing the table and watched, as if a bit enchanted, as the last one went out the door. "Carrie, you just remember that all of us can learn something from those sweet men."

Like usual, the Taurus took the *un*usual route back to Morgan, a longer route that made for a well-rounded evening with no sights twice, as though planned by Norgaard Travel. Now, in the full-moon evening, the Taurus sped down the highway, slowing like it always did for a better look as it circled past the Lower Sioux reservation casino. Grand beyond all their imagination with its size and bright lights and its parking lot filled to capacity no matter the time of day, the casino had seemingly sprung out from the land which before was only an old bingo hall surrounded by cornfields. Now even plush buses with city people came from as far away as Chicago.

Past the casino, the Taurus picked up speed as it turned onto the north road heading to Morgan, then slowed again as it passed the site for the casino's new golf course—at least that was the talk in town after the casino contacted a couple of farmers on that north side of town about buying their land. "A golf course designed by the pros"—that's how it was described just a week before in *The Redwood Gazette*. Looking out their windows now at the moonlit countryside, the guys couldn't imagine anything other than the fields of corn and soybeans and the gentle creek cutting through. "Naw, nothing's going on here yet." Hubert was the only one to comment. The others just nodded, and the car sped up again for the last few miles.

The Taurus coasted as it passed the Morgan city-limits sign and then rounded the corner at the Lutheran church. Like the end of a movie, Elmer straightened up in his seat and sighed. "Yeah, Russel, you made a nice tour of it again. We had a good meal and a real fine drive!"

"Amen. We have our own personal tour guide, with Russel here at the wheel, always making it interesting. He needs one of those *chauffeur* caps—what do you say, Russ?" Rich leaned up from the back seat and pantomimed tipping a cap.

Russ tugged down on the bill of his cap embossed "30th Infantry." "Think I'll stick to mine—works real good." He shook his head at Rich's antics, but with a smile.

Then Elmer erupted in a giggle.

"It wasn't that funny . . ."

"No, no . . . I was just thinking . . . You know what they're calling us now, don't you?" He raised his eyebrows waiting for an answer.

The others looked at Elmer with puzzled faces, even Russ who took his eyes off the road a second.

"The Gang! That's what I heard anyway, in the pool hall last week. Dorothy, she's the one who mentioned it." Elmer snickered and turned to address everyone in the car with a confident nod. "The Gang—that's us!" he said like a coach with a pumped fist to his team.

"Oh, that's what you're getting at . . . yeah, I heard that too in the barber shop this morning." Roy was eager to add what he knew. He reached up to smooth his short-cropped hair as a reminder of the conversation with Gordy the barber and Ernest Johnson, the bank president. He practically skipped home after that, even on a bad leg, so proud to be one of this group that even had a name.

"Yeah, heard it too," Hubert mumbled. "Thought maybe it was just talk."

"I even heard that some think we should support the Morgan Café instead of driving all over the county. They don't like that a bit." Elmer put that out there mostly as bait for Russ.

"Hell, that's probably just those new owners! The Café is never open when we want to go and doesn't have good food besides. And why shouldn't we make a night of it, see different things—it's a free country, isn't it?" Russ' foot got a little heavy on the foot-feed as he rounded the turn towards Vernon Avenue, so the other two in the front seat grabbed the dashboard and the three in the back grabbed the front seat to steady themselves.

"I heard that some other guys might want in on it . . . ? " Donnie's statement sounded more like a question, hoping someone would assure him that his place in the car was secure.

"Yeah, I tell them we don't have room for any more. Heck, six is all that fits in the car! Now, if a seat opens up . . . well . . . that's another story." Russ couldn't help but rub it in whenever Donnie sounded wimpish.

"Six it is!" Rich reached around to shake Donnie's hand and then the others.

"Well, we'll just let them talk, humph . . ." Hubert hadn't budged from staring out the window, but as they passed the Catholic Church, his eyes shifted.

Elmer giggled again. "Hmm . . . 'The Gang' . . . You know, that might sound *DANGEROUS* . . ." He opened his eyes wide as he drew out the word before the punch line. ". . . that is, if we were *YOUNGER!*" The car itself seemed to jiggle with delight. Even Hubert's face lit up.

The Taurus retraced its route in the sleepy town, dropping men off one by one, speeding away like a bus on a tight schedule, then settling back into Russ' garage, just as the ten-o'clock-whistle blew.

CHAPTER 11
THE COOKER

The 1987 green Buick Electra cruised down the two-lane highway, leaving the small farming town of Willmar, passing flat acres of tall corn and thick soybeans. The pavement steamed from the hot mid-day summer sun. Only an occasional car or truck shared the stretch of highway that afternoon.

"This is one day a guy can appreciate an air-conditioner, that's for darned sure. I'm usually one for rolling down the windows, but not today!" Russ in the back seat of the Buick raised his hand to feel the blast of cold air aimed high from the front vent of the car.

"It's cooling down real nice in here, guys." Elmer's oldest son, Norman, was driving. Elmer enlisted him as chauffeur because today required a special trip of nearly sixty miles to the Willmar Hospital where Hubert was recovering from his second knee replacement surgery. Since Elmer had the closest ties to Hubert from their years together on the Morgan Farmers' Elevator Board, he felt an obligation to use his car.

"Well now, what did you guys think about Hubert? Elmer took his cap off and wiped the beads of sweat from his forehead. Going on ninety-two now, Elmer got around better than most even a decade younger, even on two artificial knees, but today's heat stress was evident from his flushed face. "He didn't look too good to me, hooked up to all those contraptions. Not good at all—nope, not good at all. We should have waited another day or two to visit, don't you think?" He asked the question like one who needed to be assured.

"Naw, Hubert's tough. And I think he kind of liked us stopping by the way we did. He even smiled a little when I kidded him about the bedpan—you know, that plastic urinal gadget that looked like a water pitcher." Roy chuckled half under his breath re-playing the joke in his mind. He nudged Russ who was sitting next to him in the back seat for approval.

"Well, I'd say, that a bedpan is always funny, except when *you're* the guy that has to use it, don't you think?" Russ nudged Roy back but set up the one-liner for the whole car to hear. He grinned and waited.

"Well, wait a minute, wait a minute—a bedpan can be real handy when a guy doesn't want to get up in the middle of the night. I got real used to it when I had my knee done. What's *not* so good is there's always a nurse there to measure how much you got in it." Elmer had his head cranked to the back seat. He paused for effect, trying to hold in his amusement. "Embarrassing, that's what it is, especially when it's just a spoonful!" He turned back to face the front, wide-grinned and satisfied with the chuckles all around.

Still, Roy felt uneasy, not so sure of his hospital manners, using that joke maybe a little too soon when a guy in Hubert's condition today might be wondering whether he's going to make it or not. He peeked over his glasses to get a better look at everyone's reaction.

Russ noticed. "But you're darned right, Roy. I think that joke tickled old Hubert, even if he wasn't looking too hot with all those tubes. Yeah, made me hurt just looking at him. You bet, that was a good story, Roy, sure was."

Roy let out an exaggerated sigh and slapped his knee. "Yeah, that was a pretty good one, wasn't it? And I usually can't remember jokes!"

One by one giggles erupted at the Ole and Lena joke—the one with Ole dosed up on medication, mistaking the plastic urinal for a pitcher on his bed tray. Roy had beamed with his accomplishment to cheer up the hospital visit that afternoon and now to play it all over again, he was all the more proud. But, as the others chuckled on with their amusement, even embellishing the story with dire consequences of actual hospital mishaps, he became quiet with something of a hesitant look. He turned to watch the passing cornfields and farmsteads, and his forehead creased. "Sure makes me wonder, though, every time *I'm* in a hospital. I've been through it enough times, wondering if I'm going to make it. You never know if this is your last time . . ." His voice trailed off as he stared out the window.

"What's that you saying, Roy? You're going to the hospital and not sure you're going to make it?" Elmer turned down the fan and craned his neck to the back seat.

"No, no. I just said, you just never know when *you're* the one in the hospital, that's all." He arched his eyebrows at the sudden quiet in the car, a bit self-conscious to be the center of attention again. "But, you know—here I am today! Not too sharp, especially with numbers—but here I am today!" He sat up straight with a lively smile, as if recovered from a bout of seriousness. He turned to Russ and nudged him again. "That's why I need Russel here—he's pretty sharp with numbers. You must have got that from all those years in the grocery business, huh, Russ?" Roy was glad to change the subject.

And Russ obliged, always proud of his business skills. "Well, Roy, I always had a knack for arithmetic and keeping track of things. Plus, my dad taught me real good in the store so he could turn the business over to me when he couldn't do it anymore. Kept him in good health though and me too for that matter. Haven't been in a hospital—that is, except for in the war . . ." Russ paused, waiting for someone to ask to hear the story again.

And just that quick, Roy prompted, "How did that go again, Russel?"

"Yeah, Russel, tell that one again so Norman can here it straight from you."

The three nodded in agreement.

Russ beamed and settled back in his seat with his finger to his chin. "Well, that of course was after I'd been in the foxhole six days straight in the winter, snowing every day—no overcoat, just a blanket." His eyes drifted to a place long ago as he settled back in his seat to recount the story of his harrowing experience in Belgium, 1944. It was on Christmas Eve when he finally crawled to safety behind enemy lines. "Yes, sir, the doc pinned a tag on me and it said"—and at this point Elmer and Roy chimed in with him: "'pneumonia, bronchitis and pleurisy.'" Russ stopped a second to acknowledge the audience participation, smiled, and then continued. "So I was sent off to the Paris General Hospital for a month—that's my hospital experience. Plenty of guys I know kicked off out there in the front line, so in that way, I guess I was pretty lucky to be in the hospital." He liked ending on a positive note as if to trick anyone not listening close enough. He glanced over at Roy with a smile. "Oh, hah—and darned lucky to have one of those bedpans."

Roy and Norman chuckled being reminded of the bedpan joke, but Elmer, who seemed to turn hypnotic whenever Russ told his stories, was fixed with the horrifying memories of so long ago. "Well, Russel, you sure saw a lot of dying, I know. Ah, huh . . ." His eyes were far away, recalling the front page of the weekly *Morgan Messenger* in those war years with current listings of the state's war casualties. As for himself back then, he was just past the age to be called up for duty, so he maintained his farm with a certain patriotic diligence, for the good of the country, he liked to point out—good honest work if he couldn't be there fighting himself. He squinted as if to focus on a scene. "I just wonder how all those bodies got taken care of, hundreds of 'em every day. Can you imagine that—hundreds of 'em every day. Hundreds. I'll never forget those newsreels showing us all the dead bodies sprawled out, and you'd always think maybe you'd recognize one of 'em. Never did though . . ." The hum of the car and the air-conditioner filled the pause like an interlude building drama for a final scene. Then he added for good measure, "Just think, wouldn't our undertaker have a mess on his hands with dead bodies everywhere?" The picture now of dead bodies strewn around Morgan right there on Vernon Avenue or in Vernon Park or even in front of the church, cast a gruesome spell in the car. Their eyes darted as they each pondered the question in their private thoughts. The air conditioner churned.

"Cremation!" Roy blurted. "That's what they should have done!" He paused for just a second, surprising even himself at the outburst. Then aware of the awkward stillness from the other passengers and, as if given the okay to continue, he rattled off his informed take on the matter: ". . . It's less trouble and lots less expensive—$400, that's all it costs—that's what that cremation place charges, there down in the Cities. And that's what I've signed up for!" He took a breath and swallowed hard. Looking around at each of them still registering the topic, he added in a soft, higher-than-normal voice, "Ah, isn't that the way to go nowadays, fellas—with the high prices and all?"

Elmer and Russ couldn't help but be startled, first at the sudden change in volume and second at Roy's boldness on the subject. Even Norman gave a nod to the back seat from focusing on the road.

With no immediate comments, Roy slunk down in his seat. For the second time now on this ride, he had quieted the car. "I don't want a service either, just quick and easy, just quick and easy," he mumbled as he turned to watch the passing fields again.

Recognizing what a wild stretch it was for anyone from Morgan, let alone mild-mannered Roy Hanson, to accept a burial practice as radical as cremation, Russ felt a duty to rescue Roy. And all for the sake of economics! Customary review of the embalmed body, with follow-up on how good or bad the deceased looked, was a cornerstone of Morgan social obligations. Russ spoke up for all to hear, "Well, I have to say, Roy, that's what Lorraine wanted, and me too for that matter! You're absolutely right, Roy—it is a lot less expensive."

Roy straightened up some and took a deep breath as he listened, glad that Russ at least had picked up the cause.

"Always has irked me why families spend more than they can afford on those premier caskets with the special linings, and they do it all up real fancy when what the hell difference does it make anyhow? When you're dead, you're dead and what difference does it make whether you're in a box or burned up? Hell, I saw guys blown to smithereens and what do you suppose happened to them? I can tell you darn sure they weren't pieced together and put in a fancy box. No, sir!" Russ left no doubt with his commanding voice now that the issue had struck a nerve.

But Elmer snickered. "Ah . . . Roy, you know what they call that, don't you?"

"What? Call what?" Roy didn't see any reason for Elmer's light attitude with the current subject, overly dark that it was.

"You know, what you're talking about . . ." Elmer drew the word out, "c-r-e-m-a-t-i-o-n . . . Do you?"

"Huh?"

Now they all hung on the word and Elmer's wily smile.

"That's what I call . . . 'The Cooker!'"

The others blinked wide-eyed, their ears cocked towards Elmer waiting for him to explain. Norman shifted his eyes off the road again.

Roy's voice was thin. "The cooker?"

Then, catching on, Russ and Norman settled back with wide grins. Russ even had to choke back a laugh as he noticed Roy's eyes widen even more.

"That's right—the Cooker. A good name, don't you think?" Elmer smirked with satisfaction. "Of course, you know what you'll have to go through, huh? What they're going to do with you?"

Roy just blinked.

"Well, I'll tell you: They just throw a guy in and let him *roast* a little." Dramatizing with a bit of Vincent Price, Elmer couldn't help himself. He hunched over and peered down like looking into an oven. "Wonder if they double check that the guy's dead first . . . hmmm . . . maybe they poke you. In fact, I once heard about a guy . . ." Unable to hold back another second, he burst out in a raucous laugh which shook the entire front seat, and with that, Norman and Russ followed suit. Roy smiled but with clenched teeth and with his eyes lowered now to the tops of his knees where he noticed a fly had landed. He brushed it away.

Norman, in his role as chauffeur, had been taking it all in, enjoying the camaraderie of the old guys as usual, but this was too much fun not to join in. "Four hundred, you say, Roy? Well, here's a deal: *I'll* do it for $300! Can't be that hard. Say, Dad, we've still got that old pig roasting spit in the barn, don't we?" He jabbed his dad's arm from across the wide front seat.

Elmer nodded as he wiped his eyes. "Yeah, yeah, you're right, Norman. That probably would work just fine—in fact, perfect as 'The Cooker.'"

"And, Dad, we could even put an ad in the *Messenger* and make a few bucks on the side. Probably more people than just our friend Roy here would want to get our good deal. A guy wouldn't even have to be shipped to the Cities to get fried up—he could just stay here nice and comfortable in Morgan."

"And, Roy, we'd be real careful to make sure you were *dead* first."

Russ bit down on his lip as he watched the entertainment in the front seat, all the while keeping an eye on Roy, who wasn't a bit amused and seemed more concentrated now on whether that fly showed up on his knee again. The comic frenzy had Norman and Elmer doubled over with amusement so that at one point the car swerved onto the gravel shoulder, kicking up a trail of dust. That got Roy's attention enough that he straightened up and looked out just in time to see the gravel flying.

"Whoa! Just lucky for us we have an empty stretch of road this afternoon, don't you agree, Roy? Huh?" Russ gave Roy a friendly poke on the arm.

Roy turned from watching the cloud of dust and managed a tight smile. "Yeah, you're right, Russ—we're lucky, that's for sure." Then as the car settled back on the pavement, Norman and Elmer settled back too, grinning happily with themselves.

"Ha, ha . . . okay, you guys win," Roy managed in a loser voice. He resumed his watch beyond the cornfield to the horizon, wavy from the heat, and under his breath, he repeated, "The Cooker . . . the Cooker . . . the Cooker" with the rhythm of the sectioned pavements.

The big Buick glistened in the baking sun as it cut through the farm country heading back to Morgan.

"You can turn that fan up again."

The sweltering heat continued into the next day so that, even though it was Friday and usually a busy shopping day before the weekend, Morgan's Vernon Avenue was empty, except for an occasional shopper darting into the air-conditioned Super Valu, or the farmers and merchants stopping in for their usual break at the air-conditioned pool hall. On days like this, the townspeople chose to stay at home, cooler inside with shades drawn and fans set on high. The weatherman on WCCO Radio promised a break in the weather soon.

The pool hall's big window air conditioner whirred tirelessly through breakfast and lunch and now mid-afternoon coffee. Russ got up from his stool at the counter and stopped at the table where Elmer, Roy and Rich were playing "Merry Widow" with the retired school custodian, Clayton Gustafson. Clayton and Russ were both in the class of '28, and Clayton and his wife, Lucille, had been Russ's neighbors to the west since the fifties. Rich looked up from his cards with his usual generous smile, "Say, Russel, hang around a minute, and we'll make room for one more here. We'll get a game going where we can play five."

"Here, you take my place, Russel. I'm not doing so good anyway." Roy started to back up his chair. "Don't know why I'm not getting the cards today, just not in the game, I guess. It's probably the heat."

"No, no, Roy you stay put. I'm on my way home but just thought I'd check in on old Rich here, since he didn't ride along with us yesterday to visit Hubert." He patted Rich's shoulder. "Looks like you're feeling okay, Richard?"

"Oh, sure, Russ—just another bout of dizziness but it's from those dang medications. You can feel lucky that you don't have to take that stuff—gets a guy all messed up. I'm good now though." Rich turned back to look at his cards and did a double-take. "And look at here, looks like I'm going to win this game!" He laid down his hand and then folded his arms across his chest as he leaned back on his chair with a smug grin. The other three groaned.

"Well, now I *am* ready to leave." Roy tossed his cards back onto the pile. I'll see you guys tonight though." He stood up to leave and straightened his cap.

"Yeah, I've got a couple of bookkeeping things to tend to at home before we head out for supper. Five-thirty, I guess, is when we're meeting in front of the Café. Right, guys? And, Rich, you're feeling good enough to go?"

"Oh, you betcha, Russel—can't keep this good horse down!" Rich had that familiar twinkle in his eye again. "Anyway, I need some decent food—those lonely Meals-on-Wheels don't *quite* match up to us guys sitting around a table, even at a *lousy* restaurant!"

Rich's infectious laugh always managed to tickle Roy, even on a bad-card day. "Ha-ha . . . lousy. You're right though—even those lousy restaurants aren't so bad."

Clayton, being the outsider in the bunch, just smiled as he listened to the banter, feeling more than a little envious of what seemed the most prestigious group in Morgan these days. "Say, you guys are getting around a lot, I hear, hitting all the towns around? Going out at least a couple times a week, huh? And they say your car is full now?" He had a knack for fishing out details.

"You bet," Russ sensed the intrigue, ". . . got them all wondering what we're up to—never know just *where* we'll show up, or *when*. We like to keep them guessing, don't we, boys?"

"Yes, sir."

"You bet, we do."

"Yup!"

"Now take you for example, Clayton: You've got Lucille to make you a good home-cooked meal. Nothing beats that. But us, well, we bounce around from, like Rich says here, one restaurant to another, some lousy." He winked at Elmer, Roy and Rich, who in turn winked at each as if they knew a secret password. Elmer, in a raspy sort of under-cover voice interjected, "We're known as . . . 'The Gang.'"

But his eyes gave away his delight with the new fame, and he began to chuckle just saying the name again, of course prompting chuckles all around the table.

Clayton nodded but with an almost worrisome look. "As a matter of fact, I have been hearing that name just about everywhere I go these days—'The Gang.' Even at *church*!"

"Church, you say? Well, I'd say that *church* is as good as any place to be mentioned, don't you think?" Russ loved to turn things around. "Right now though, I've got to get to that bookwork." He glanced at his watch. "But I'll be in front of the café at five-thirty sharp, so . . ." He paused to do his impression of Elmer. ". . . '*The Gang*' better be there on time!" Loving every minute of piece-mealing the information to someone like Clayton who tended to share information around town, he spun around like a kid as he headed for the door, almost dizzy from the adrenaline. He hollered back, "Elmer, you better call Donnie and remind him. It'll be *five* of us tonight . . . but we'll be back to six in no time when Hubert gets out of the hospital."

At five-twenty-five Russ pulled into the parking space in front of the Morgan Café, turned off the ignition and settled back in his seat, satisfied that *he* was early. He was also curious about this new pick-up arrangement. After all, he hadn't complained—it was Rich who suggested that the least they could do for all Russ's taxiing would be to meet at a designated place. The idea seemed reasonable enough when they discussed it last week. Now, on the other hand, parked here waiting smack dab on Vernon Avenue for all to see, Russ had second thoughts: "Isn't this like fuel for the old biddies? We might as well broadcast our comings and goings over KNSJ. Before long old Viola Kepson from the *Messenger* will be getting the scoop for her "News about Town" column." He shrugged, then nodded an okay to himself: "So what? Let them talk. Why shouldn't we get out of town to see other things and make a night of it?" He drummed his fingers on the steering wheel. "And why the hell would we want to eat at the Café anyway? The cooking just never was the same after Margaret left."

He purposely had his air-conditioner turned off with the window rolled down, even though the temperature was still in the eighties, knowing soon enough he'd have to crank out the frigid air as soon the guys were in the car. Right now he preferred the hot summer smells tied to memories of long ago when Vernon Avenue was bustling with shoppers on a summer night. He nodded a greeting to Pearl Johnson and Agnes Ziegenhagen as they walked by on the sidewalk and into the cafe. "Pearl . . . Agnes . . ." They smiled.

"Hello, Russel," they sang together in soprano, their eyes darting around the car to be sure they saw everything there was to see. Both were members of the stricter Lutheran church in town, Zion Lutheran, known for its rigid tenets, like the no-communion-to-out-siders rule which riled Russ to no end—and they both were talkers. The café door closed behind them, but Russ noticed that Agnes looked back over her shoulder, still with that polite smile.

At five-thirty-two, both cars pulled up alongside Russ—Elmer in his Buick with Roy and Rich, and Donnie in his Bronco. But as Russ nodded hello, he noticed something unusual going on with the Buick: Roy's door was open, and he was half out of the car even before Elmer came to a complete stop. Without even a nod to Russ, Roy hurried into the café, head down. "What the heck?" Russ mouthed to Elmer.

The others got out and Elmer walked around to Russ's window. "Old Roy complained that he wasn't feeling so good—said he'd make a stop at the men's room before we leave. He won't be long so we'll just get in your car so we're ready to go."

"Well, he sure looked like something was ailing him, that's for darned sure. He looked okay this afternoon playing cards there at the pool hall. Did he complain then?"

"Naw, just now when we were driving over here—said he was really hot. But you know how the weather's been lately." Elmer shifted his cap back and wiped his brow. His cheeks were flushed.

"Well, you guys hop in, and I'll get my cooler going. If it's just a stop for the can, he won't be long." Russ rolled his window up, as the three shoved into the back seat.

"We'll leave the front seat for Roy so he has more air."

What seemed like long minutes went by as the four sat waiting. The air conditioner, at first welcome, soon felt like a noisy intruder, as the seconds plodded. Russ looked at his watch. "You guys stay put—I'm going to check on him and see what the heck's taking so long." Always nimble, he was out of the car just like that, leaving the others without time to respond.

Walking to the back of the café, Russ had to pass directly by the long table where he noticed Pearl and Agnes again, along with several other women he recognized from Zion. Their eyes followed him as he made his way to the men's restroom door. He knocked and whispered, "Roy . . . Roy? Are you okay in there?" He listened. Then louder, "Roy!" He rapped again. The women continued their conversation but all with their heads turned to watch the more-interesting activity at the men's restroom door.

"Oh . . . it's you, Russ . . . I think it's just . . . another one of those . . . those spells I get every so often." The voice was very different—strained and weak with heavy breaths. ". . . Just be a minute here . . . while I cool down a little with some of this . . . auhh, cold water on my face . . ."

Russ heard the faucet run full blast and waited with his ear to the door. He tried the knob but the door was locked. "Open the door, Roy. Let's see how you're doing. Roy? ROY?"

He heard a click and opened the door. Roy was sitting on the stool with his head down, hands clasped behind his neck, his hair tossed and wet. He looked up at Russ with a weak grin but heavy eyes, "I think I'll skip going with you guys tonight—just not hungry anymore . . . Just a spell though, that's all it is." Russ grabbed a handful of paper towels, wetted them, and handed them to Roy. "Here, hold these on your head. I'm calling an ambulance, just to be on the safe side." He disappeared out into the café.

By the time the ambulance door closed, some twenty minutes later, a small crowd had gathered on the sidewalk in front of the Morgan

Café—the town cop, the clerk from Shortie's Hardware who had just locked up for the day and was heading home, a couple of boys on bicycles, and the new mechanic from the Texaco station just leaving the liquor store next door. The Zion Lutheran ladies group remained inside the café, huddled by the front window. Elmer, Donnie, and Rich, who had been holding watch at the ambulance since it arrived, formed a sort-of receiving line as Roy was loaded into the ambulance on a stretcher. Russ handled last minute details with the paramedic, and then the ambulance sped off for Sleepy Eye Hospital, fifteen miles away.

"Well, guys," Russ started the engine and then looked at his watch, "you can bet that the hospital will be busy with old Roy for quite a while. You know how it is with the doctors and tests—always take so damned long. We could be sitting there half the night before we know anything. So, we might as well eat first and check on Roy after things have calmed down a bit. How's that for a plan?" He looked around at the others, Elmer now occupying Roy's designated seat in the front with the air-conditioner aimed at his face.

The three, still numb from the unusual events in their otherwise usual evening out, just nodded and grunted an approval.

"Well, okay then." Convinced by their vacant faces that it was up to him to move things along, Russ threw out options: "Let's see, New Ulm is the closest restaurant in the direction of the hospital. There isn't anything in Sleepy Eye, that's for sure. Wish they'd have something open at night, damn it—always closed up tighter than a drum just when a guy could use a restaurant right there!" Russ pulled his wet collar out from his neck and sat forward in his seat to let the cool air slide down his back. He felt an uneasiness just sitting still so he revved the motor and backed up. "Hmm . . . wonder what the heck is going on with Roy . . . he told me he has these spells every so often . . ."

"Sure, Russ, you go ahead and pick a place. You're the driver so you decide. Gosh, it's still hot out there." Even Rich was out of words.

Russ made a left turn off Vernon Avenue and headed to New Ulm on Highway 68. Far out ahead, just at the horizon, they could see the back of the ambulance, traveling almost in tandem—then it faded into the hazy sky, but no one commented.

Elmer finally spoke. "You know, I remember a couple days ago Roy complained he wasn't feeling too good so we didn't play cards that day. But yesterday he sure was himself when we visited Hubert, even joking—remember that? We all had a good laugh, remember? And I know he was looking forward to tonight. He even said so this afternoon at the pool hall."

The others nodded in agreement. One by one they joined in with their versions on Roy's behavior over the last couple of weeks, concluding that he was no complainer by any standard and that the heat and humidity combination were rough on everyone the last couple of days.

Elmer seemed satisfied that he hadn't missed a clue. "You know, come to think of it, I've *never* heard him complain, even after that stroke."

Russ had just turned into the Mr. Steak parking lot and was circling the parked cars with his eyes, intent on the perfect spot. "Well, at least we know he's getting checked out. I was impressed with those . . . what you call them . . . paramedics? Whatever they are . . . they really knew what they were doing, seemed like to me." He slowed down further. "Ah hah, there's someone leaving right by the front door." He swung the car wide and slid into the space. Turning off the engine, he checked his watch with a look of satisfaction. "Yes, sir, gentlemen— our friend Roy will be ready for some company by the time we're done here."

They toasted Roy with their brandy sevens at Mr. Steak and ordered their ribeyes and baked potatoes with full salad bar and coffee. With lightened moods and full stomachs, the conversation switched to Twins baseball and time-worn WCCO jokes—most of them Roy's favorites. It was a car full of laughs and one-liners that headed to Sleepy Eye Hospital just as the sun was setting, cooler now. Russ opened his window. "Let's try some fresh air."

The four men marched up to the information desk, like a welcoming committee. "We're here to see Roy Hanson. Ah, he came here by ambulance earlier this evening after a little spell at the Morgan Cafe." Russ fumbled in his billfold for Roy's insurance information he was sure he'd need to pull out again. "I have his power of attorney, and all of us here, well, we're his buddies. Roy is one of the Gang, from Morgan, that is." Russ exchanged confident nods with the other three.

The young woman's eyes opened wide. "Yes . . . just a moment please." She left the desk and disappeared down the hall through wide doors labeled "E.R."

Within a minute she appeared again, but with a tall middle-age man, glasses and fair skinned with a mustache, a stethoscope around his neck and a long white coat that made him look even taller. The four men looked up at the doctor.

"I understand, gentlemen, you are here to see Roy Hanson?"

They nodded.

"Well, I'm very sorry to tell you that Mr. Hanson died of a massive coronary attack on the way to the hospital. There was nothing more we could do when he arrived. Are any of you a relative?

The four dropped their mouths, then looked at each other in a questioning sort of stare, shaking their heads in unison.

"Family? Does he have any family?"

They stared up at him. Then Russ finally spoke. "No, doctor. I'm afraid not. It's just us—I guess we're his family."

CHAPTER 12
THE LOVE BOAT

Wilbur Best filled that sixth seat in the car, the enviable, available seat now that Roy was gone. He was the logical choice, living just next door to Rich and a recent widower. Pathetic really was how he had looked when he waved as the guys drove off from Rich's house each week and one of the reasons actually that the group decided to meet at the Vernon Avenue pickup, to avoid that downcast look. But the drawback, the main mark against him to Russ's way of thinking, was that Wilbur was a teetotaler. Russ made it clear to the group in no uncertain terms that *no one* in his car would be casting judgment on a simple whisky sour, *no one*— the others could only agree. But Rich with his expansive heart cast his vote for Wilbur, and that in the end was good enough for Russ. So it was, that Wilbur, the soft-spoken, provincial Methodist, whose idea of a good time might sooner be a Bible study group, found himself among the Gang from Morgan aboard a cruise ship in the Caribbean.

"Gosh darn! Isn't this exactly how it looks on *Love Boat*? Like a hotel on water, and a heck-of-a-big one—more than twice as many people on this boat as in all of Morgan. Can you believe it? And did you see the captain shaking hands with that real good-looking blonde gal and her man? Both looked like movie stars. Some big bucks there, I'll bet." Russ held the elevator door open while Elmer, Hubert and Wilbur, each maneuvering a wheeling-suitcase tipsy-turvy, squeezed in. Their luggage somehow ended in the middle so they stood in a circle facing each other. A young couple, waiting too, opted to catch the next elevator and waved them on.

"Guess we're lucky that it's just the four of us cramming into one of these little elevators and getting around this big bruiser of a boat." Russ noticed the others were showing some signs of fatigue as they now leaned on the handles of their luggage.

Elmer, Wilbur, Russ, and Hubert at the cruise banquet.

"Yeah, I can see what you mean, Russel." Elmer wiped his forehead and then leaned on the handle again. The other two nodded in agreement, although they seemed preoccupied studying the mirrored ceiling of the elevator.

Russ hit the R button for "Riviera"—the bottom button of the elevator choices. Riviera seemed like an exotic name for the lowest deck on the ten-story cruise liner. The elevator beeped, the door started to close but caught the back of Wilbur's jacket and opened again, then stalled—another beep, another stall, finally the door closed with the four readjusted and huddled closer. "Hell, next time we'll take the stairs."

"Maybe *you* will, Russel, but not me." Elmer's face was flushed, his cap slightly off center and his shirt only half tucked in now after the effects of a long day traveling from Minnesota to Florida. His tired eyes still twinkled. Travel for the four actually started the previous day when the Russ drove them to a daughter's home in the Twin Cities where they stayed the night, spread out about the house here and there on an extra bed, a couple of couches, so they could catch the early flight to Miami the next morning. Tough old guys by anyone's definition you might say—for traveling requires a certain flexibility often not suited for slackers. Elmer wiped his forehead with the back of his hand. "I just hope our room is close to the elevator."

But it wasn't. The four set out through the long, busy hallways, making their way to the interior rooms toward the back of the ship about midway from the elevators, making one wrong turn, then stopping twice to rest, Elmer and Wilbur, now both with red faces and both sitting on their suitcases. "It's a good thing we didn't leave our suitcases with that porter fella—at least this way we have a place to sit."

Hubert pulled out a collapsible stool from his bag and sat on that. "Yeah, cheaper too. Those tips can mount up on a deal like this." He had some authority to speak on the topic since he was the experienced traveler of the bunch.

As the others rested, Russ paced the hallway, looking at the framed photos of lush islands, sea life, and ocean sunsets. "Yeah, well, maybe a porter wouldn't have been such a bad idea this time.

Sure would be a hell of a note if you guys can't even get to the room. I'd sure as heck flag one down right now if I'd see one." He scanned the hallway one way and then the other, but only saw other passengers preoccupied with finding their rooms. A mid-aged couple passed by with polite smiles. Then a young couple, looking fresh out of college, asked if anything was wrong. Russ was quick to assure them, "Oh, hello there . . . no, just resting a bit . . . just taking a break . . . sure is a big ship, this Fantasy . . . you too . . . have a nice day . . ."

He led the way about three yards ahead of the others down the last long corridor. "Here we are—Room R-127, that's us." Russ double-checked his key, then parked his suitcase matter-of-factly on the carpet and smiled as if opening a present when he heard the lock click as he turned the key and opened the door. A whiff of scented air, like a mixture of tropical fruit and cheap air freshener wafted out of the small narrow room. They bunched up at the door to look in: Bunk beds lined one wall, leaving the opposite side for a tiny built-in desk and a sitting area with a small bench seat and two white plastic-formed chairs on metal legs. A television hung from the corner ceiling like in a hospital room. What appeared to be a window was draped in a printed fabric to match the mauve carpet, and a valance hid a light fixture to cast a bright mood down over the drapery.

Russ led the way into the room, nodding an "okay" as he looked about, pacing through his mental checklist and grinning wide. "Yes, sir, looks like everything we need anyway—not big that's for darned sure, but we're not going to be spending much time in here anyway. Looks and smells clean." He ran his hand over the desk top. "Let's see what we've got for a bathroom . . ."

"Hold on, hold on . . . just a minute here, *I'll* see how the toilet works." Hubert pushed past Russ to make a quick exit into the bathroom and slammed the door. Elmer and Wilbur both still red-faced hurried over and plopped themselves into the plastic-molded chairs.

"Okay, Hubert, you can report on the plumbing," Russ hollered at the bathroom door. But now distracted and with a look of skepticism, he eyed something peculiar across the room. He walked over to the drapery to peek behind it. Was that a window there? Just to make double sure the room was as described in his brochure, that there really *wasn't* a porthole, he was puzzled. After all, an actual porthole would mean they were in an exterior room, which he was sure they weren't, and that they would be paying a stiffer price, which he reasoned they darned-well better not be. Pulling back the drape, what he saw was a rather nice mural of palm trees and aquamarine ocean, painted right there on the wall in the shape of a porthole. "Not a bad idea," he muttered, with a smirk. "Hey, look at this, boys—our own private view of the ocean!"

"Well, I'll be. Sure enough, a painting—real nice."

"And the weather never changes. Hee hee."

Russ dropped the curtain back into place and began to pace the tight quarters. It was the bed options he was surveying now. His eyes moved from one set of bunk beds to the other, up then down, up then down. "Hmmm."

KABOOM! SUSHHH-WHIRRR . . . All three spun their heads to the bathroom door, their eyes popping wide open like runaway window shades. They listened . . . just silence . . . then, a faucet running . . . then the handle turned and the narrow door flipped open. Out came Hubert, even more gangly-looking in proportion to the small door. With his heavy jaw and straight face, he muttered, "Loud—but it works," then proceeded to sit down on one of the lower bunks which required that either he crouch to fit, or remove his cap. He crouched.

The other three erupted in giggles. Even modest Wilbur.

Russ wiped his brow in relief, ever vigilant since the trip began for any catastrophes waiting in the wings. A heavy responsibility, that's how he figured it, especially now that the trip was well underway with no turning back. He squelched a deep sigh, then tried to look serious before giving Hubert a gibe. "Holy smokes, Hubert! That was a hell of a sound! We thought the bottom of the ship dropped out for sure! You sure you didn't break anything in there?"

"Was it . . . a bomb?" Elmer slapped his knee, tears now welling in his eyes. Wilbur just giggled at the floor.

"Yeah, yeah, very funny. You try it out and see how you do with it." The ends of Hubert's mouth turned up in a sly grin. He took off his cap and laid back on the bunk cautiously, stretching out one long leg, then the other, his shoes hanging over the end. "What I want to know is: What are we going to do about these beds?"

That got Russ and Elmer going again, picturing now—thanks to Hubert's demonstration—the reality of bedtime scenarios for the next week: four old men straddled on bunk beds in a room the size of a closet—and with an explosive toilet. Wilbur, not knowing for sure just when to laugh and when to get serious—because after all, these bunk beds *were* a serious matter and a matter that had been on his mind since setting foot in this room, not to mention, and above all, he wanted to be respective of his bunkmates—smiled, then cleared his throat and in his small voice said like a school headmaster, "We could draw names . . . that would be the fair thing to do . . ."

"Hell, let's see which of us can even get *up* there!" Set into action, Russ stepped over to the bed, put his foot on the first wrung of the little ladder and started up with a spring in his step like a young private. "Let's see . . . just three steps . . . then you get your knee up here . . . and . . . then flop down. Whew. There!" He lay back on the pillow, his heart pumping excitement. Noticing how close he was to the ceiling, he reached with his arm to confirm that he could touch it. "No sitting up here, that's for darned sure. But I got to tell you, this is luxury compared to the *Queen Mary* in '44 . . ." He stared at the ceiling with his hands in a prayer position across his chest. ". . . there we were, thirteen guys in a room normally for two. Can you believe that? Thirteen guys in a room about like this—oh, maybe a little bigger." His eyes drifted for a second, recalling like only yesterday a couple of G.I. faces from that room so long ago.

"Russel, I hate to say it, but I don't think I can make it up there with these artificial knees of mine." Elmer had his hands on his knees, shaking his head, as he looked up at Russ.

At that, Russ was brought back to focus at the ceiling again and then to his present bunkmates. He turned to look down at Elmer. "Well, Elmer, I had a notion about that when we were waiting for Hubert—before that *bomb* went off, that is . . ." he chuckled automatically, like the word "bomb" would forever bring that scene to mind. "How about if you and Hubert here with the artificial knees have the bottom bunks, and Wilbur and I with our regular knees have the top ones? Wilbur, you do have your own knees still, don't you?"

Wilbur startled by the direct question, put his hands on his knees and looked down at them as if trying to remember. Then he looked back at Russ and grinned proudly, "Yes, Russel, I've had these eighty-two years so far."

"Well there you are guys. Now let's see you get up there, Wilbur." Russ got up on his elbow so he could watch.

"Oh, boy, Russel, if you think so, I'll give it a try. I'll just have to take my time." A little wobbly, Wilbur got up from the chair and grabbed the ladder to the bed. "My knees stiffen up, that's all, even from that little bit of sitting. And my bifocals, well, they sometimes fool me too with steps, like this ladder here. But as long as I have something to hold on to, I think I'll make it just fine." He took the two steps on the ladder without much effort, but instead of hoisting himself then with his knee onto the mattress, he took one more step, teetered a bit—enough that Elmer and Hubert below flung their arms out as if to catch him—then leaned over so he could brace his foot against the metal frame, then shoved himself on his belly until he was centered on the bed. "Ohh, my goodness . . ." he grunted, "I'll do better next time." He smiled up at the ceiling and then across at Russ, "but I made it!" They clapped, and Wilbur smiled bigger than he had since before his wife, Elsie, died.

Satisfied now that they had passed a fitness test of sorts in their new quarters for the next six days, the four old guys now settled into Stateroom R-127, the Riviera Deck, just above the water line on the ten-story cruise ship named *Fantasy*, with the view of painted palm trees and aquamarine ocean just behind the drapery. It was their little piece of the Caribbean, their new world with beautiful people, luxury, wealth, exotic places, and tropical weather. This new world of ten decks including five swimming pools, two casinos, three stages, two dance floors, two shopping malls, a gymnasium with spas and workout rooms, five bars, and two grand dining rooms was quite enough for these old men from rural Minnesota, to wander and absorb in those six days. And, foremost, it was their opportunity to choose anything on the menu.

"I'll have the swordfish tonight please, always wanted to try that." Russ took his last bite of shrimp cocktail and handed the empty goblet to the waiter. "Thank you very much. You put on quite a nice spread here."

"Yes, sir. We're proud of our ship line. Our galley is the finest, sir." The young waiter was handsome with his dark hair slicked back and white uniform, and he had a friendly smile and bright dark eyes. He especially liked serving this table with the four old men, an out-of-the-ordinary travel group to say the least on this cruise tagged "the party boat." Like kids in a candy store, they stared longingly at the menu unable to decide among so many choices, only to be reminded each time that they could have anything and everything. The menu was magical, and he their personal waiter, the magician. And big eaters they were, savoring each bite, sampling, ordering more, knowing for this one week they would not have that irksome worry: a bill to divvy up. "We're just the same as everyone else," Russ reminded the other three when they'd get to their room each night. "They don't know if we have a million bucks or not. Yes, siree, this is the way to go."

Little did they know that in fact they did stand out. Two mid-aged couples also sat at this assigned table for the week, one from New Jersey and one from Canada, "pleasant-enough but not real sociable," as Russ first described them. But although initially just intrigued by their strange dinner mates, even embarrassed a little and privately amused, they soon were captivated by "the four gentlemen from Minnesota," as the term of endearment spread throughout the ship, and even a sister ship, that week. "Can we help you, gentlemen?" or "Do you need directions, gentlemen?" or "Do you need some assistance getting around, gentlemen?" or any variation of offers to help were the norm as the old men dined and made their way around, up and down the cruise ship, tipping their farmer caps as they greeted their admirers.

But that sort of attention worked both ways for Russ—like a back-handed compliment. "You'd think we were half dead." He fidgeted at the desk and for the umpteenth time leafed through the brochure entitled "Fantasy Land Tours." "Just look at these pictures. You don't see any old duffers like us, that's for darned sure. Couples, that's what you see, couples . . . and mostly young ones at that. Hell, our grandkids are older than some of them." He stopped at the page entitled "Exotic Mexican Waterfall Tour." "That climb we did to the waterfall yesterday, there at the Mexican place, what was that name again . . ." He adjusted his bifocals and looked closely at the page, sounding out the name. "Coz-u-mel. Well, Elmer, I thought your face was going to *bust*, you were so red with the heat and all those steps, sitting there on that rock, and only halfway up, too yet. Hell of a climb. I was damned-near ready to call an ambulance . . . if there even was one . . . in Coz-u-mel, whatever. What if you'd kicked off right then and there?" Russ looked up from the brochure, waiting for a reaction from the others, but instead got only blank looks from the three intent on the television—slightly sunburned, slightly wind-blown old guys in Bermuda shorts, two down to their undershirts, watching a re-run of "Green Acres." He felt a tinge of guilt for even mentioning frailties, seeing them now—after all they were troopers. And no one had kicked off, yet.

Russ resumed his conversation with himself, but loud enough for them to hear over the television. "I know, I know, even a young fella can't take too much of this hot, muggy weather when he's used to the cold in Minnesota. Darn it though . . . I'd like to see more people our age getting out and doing stuff." He continued leafing through the brochure. "Yeah, these pictures don't show guys like us." Then he dropped his voice. "And by the way, where *are* all the widows?"

Lulled by the TV, Elmer finally chimed in going back to Russ's first comment, "Well, *half* dead isn't so bad, Russel," and then he snickered. "After all, here we are on a big boat in the Caribbean in the middle of winter. Who knows—they're probably having a snowstorm at home, and we're sitting here in our Bermuda shorts, think of that." He held one leg out to admire a hint of sunburn on his pasty skin. "Right now though, I'm going to take a little snooze and plan what I'm going to order for dinner." Elmer yawned as he slid his shoes off and lay down on his bed.

Wilbur turned the volume down on the TV. "At least we'll have something to tell our kids. My daughter over in Milwaukee—you know, Beverly, my oldest—she works for one of those big companies. She's always worried about me sitting around alone at home. In fact, she wants me to come live with her." He smiled like a kid. "Well, I wonder what she's thinking this week about me on this big trip." He buttoned the top button of his shirt, smoothed his hair down, and picked up his cap from the top bunk. "We have a couple hours before dinner, is that correct?

They all checked their watches and nodded.

"Well, I'm going to find one of those deck chairs not too far away from the elevator just up three floors on that Atlantic deck—I think that's what it is. That's a good place to watch people or nap, either way. How about it. Hubert? We can take our time getting there. Russel? How about it?" He stood ready for action in the center of the room, proud to be the one initiating a plan.

"Yeah, yeah, I suppose I'll go with you." Hubert looked tired, his face particularly long and drawn, but he grabbed his shirt from the bed and put it on. "I just want to look out at the sky awhile— they say that's what can help ease the stomach and that wobbly feeling. That's what Clara and I would do on these cruises. I'm about ready to get back to good old Minnesota winter again—that snowstorm you mentioned, Elmer, sounds pretty good to me." He positioned his cap just so, and the two shuffled to the door.

"Come on, Russel."

"Naw, you two go ahead." Russ drummed his fingers on the desk, preoccupied now with his own plan. "I'm going to nose around a little. Only a couple days left, and I'd like to see all there is to see on this darned ship. Got a couple places in mind I haven't been yet, and I still have some film left in my camera."

"Okay, then, Russel. Just remember: Stay out of trouble." Wilbur giggled, pleased with himself now that he was getting the hang of the group dynamics. Teasing was a social aspect that didn't come easy for him. But he had taken to heart the advice of his good neighbor Rich just before leaving on the cruise. That's when Rich put his hand on Wilbur's shoulder and in earnest said, "Wilbur, my friend, just loosen up—think of it like riding loose in the saddle," and then Rich demonstrated by pretending a light hold on invisible reins. After that advice, Wilbur sensed an awakening within himself, though modest, by the mere delight in even hinting at trouble. "Oh, and don't do anything Rich wouldn't do! Isn't that what he told us before we left?" Wilbur shook his index finger in fun.

Hubert just nodded with a grunt and pushed Wilbur on through the door. "Yeah, Russel, we'll see you and Elmer before supper."

Wilbur waved back, all grins. "See you guys later!"

"Don't worry. I'll follow Rich's advice. You betcha." Russ waved them off and smiled, shaking his head at just how sturdy these guys were, despite their differences. "Yeah, Rich," he said under his breath, "we won't do anything you wouldn't do yourself. You would kick up your heels, I know." The door closed, and he turned to make another pitch with Elmer, but by then Elmer had curled up comfortably on his bed and was making those quiet raspy noises of someone falling asleep.

Russ tiptoed to his bed to grab his cap and camera and eased out the door on his mission to explore, sensing almost a rush of teenage independence. Now alone, he walked at his usual brisk pace, clipping along with that nondescript whistle under his breath. First on his agenda: the purser's information desk three decks up.

There at the glossy white counter with a gold-embossed "Purser" sign overhead Russ spread out his map of the *Fantasy* while he waited for the clerk to finish her telephone conversation. She looked professional enough and even a bit glamorous with her make-up and bright pink uniform, but she didn't look much older than his granddaughters and, from what he could hear, seemed to be chatting on a personal call. He thumped his fingers and cleared his throat. After a long minute, she hung up the receiver and turned to him. "Yes, good afternoon, sir. What can I do for you?"

"And good afternoon to you, miss." He tipped his cap. "Ah, I'd like to see the area where a guy can take a stroll."

"A stroll?" She tilted her head. "You mean a walk?" Her eyebrows raised and she seemed to get up on her tiptoes with the question.

"Sure, sure—a walk, guess that's what we say nowadays." He could tell that he got her attention—her eyebrows were still raised. "You see, I was on one of these ships back in '44—that was during the war, you know. The *Queen Mary*, that was the ship. I was nothing but a private, but it was my job to guard Churchill when he took his daily stroll. That's what he called it, his 'stroll.'" Russ smiled matter-of-factly at the girl, confident that his explanation would produce an enthusiastic response. Then after that enthusiastic response, he would launch into an engaging conversation about World War II and how it was that he, a small-town GI was chosen to guard the promenade deck so that the prime minister of Britain might take his daily "stroll" as he and his family traveled back home on the *Queen Mary*—that very ship carrying thousands of troops overseas in what were the planning stages for the soon to follow invasion of Europe.

"Ah, huh, yes, sir. I'm not familiar with, Church—well, you say?" She crinkled her forehead as she twisted her finger around a strand of hair.

"Churchill. Winston *Churchill*," Russ snapped the name. "He was the head of Britain. Always had a cigar, heavy-set . . ."

"Ah, huh." She smiled which was more like a programmed response to move along with the conversation. She looked down at Russ's map and pointed to the various areas: "Yes, the promenade deck—here—offers some nice viewing along the bar areas near the dance floors. Otherwise, I'd say that the sun deck—here—offers the best place for a walk, there next to the jogging track. Or, then there's the sports deck—here. Those are the top three decks, sir." She quickly circled the areas on his map with her bright pink marker.

"Okay . . ." Russ studied the circled areas and added his own notes, "I'll see what I can find . . ." He clicked his pen and secured it in his front shirt pocket, then folded the map slowly as he added, "You know that *Churchill* walked for an hour every day, smoking his cigar of course. He was the head guy in Britain, our ally."

"Really, ah huh," she offered with little enthusiasm. "Oh, excuse me, sir—I need to answer this phone . . ." Eager now to move along, she twiddled her fingers in a goodbye as she picked up the receiver. "Good afternoon, Purser's Desk, Candy speaking . . ."

"Well, okay then . . . Candy" he muttered to himself as he picked up his map and turned to leave, noticing only then that two couples, middle-aged, were waiting in line behind him. They were nudging each other and whispering—the two women were giddy with what seemed to be secret information. As Russ stepped aside, one of the women put her face close to his and spoke extraordinarily loud, slow, and in a southern drawl, with her red lips sounding out each word: "Oh, excuse us, sir, but aren't you one of those gentlemen from Minnesota that we've been hearing about?"

Russ took a step back. "Well, yes—I guess that's what they've been calling us. Just *why* you've been hearing about us, don't ask me, but yes, we're from Minnesota." He had always been leery of southern drawls, especially after one of his daughters divorced an impulsive Texan. But, not to hold that against this stranger and cruise-mate, he managed a polite smile. Who knows, he thought, they too might be checking on a place to stroll.

"Well good for you. Bless your heart. We want you to know what an inspiration it is to see men, you know, *your* age having some fun—ah, don't we, Donald?" She looked at her husband, then the other couple, and the three nodded together in agreement. The other woman apparently unable to match her friend's words just cooed. Just then the clerk hung up the phone and turned to the group. "Next. May I help you?"

"Oh, why yes! We'd like to sign up for those dance lessons—the swing class!" At that, Russ scooted aside so that the eager couples could edge up to the glossy counter to take care of their dance business. Never one himself to take to dance steps, he wondered for that second if he could intrigue them with a stroll instead, but, seeing their enthusiasm, thought better of it. The woman with the red lips seemed to be in full charge and intent on pointing to a picture of dancers in her brochure opened to the page entitled "Self Improvement." "Here, on this page," she pointed out, ". . . it says 'Swing lessons—no experience necessary' . . ." But she kept her eye on Russ and as he turned to leave, she held her finger on the page and waved to him. "Bye-bye now, sweetie . . . ya'll have fun, you and those other fine, fine Gentlemen from Minnesota!" The other woman cooed again.

Russ tipped his cap and came out with a cheery, "You bet we will!" But as he turned and walked away, he muttered to himself in a fake drawl, "Yeah, imagine that—'men your age' having fun. I wonder what age that is—probably half-dead!"

Likely it was the combined effect of her comment along with the young clerk's clueless stare at the mention of the war that got his goat, and got it good. He was in one grumpy mood. He muttered all the way down the long corridor to the elevator. "Heck . . . one guy's sleeping in the room on an absolutely perfect day, two are half-asleep on some deck chairs, one of them seasick . . . it's lucky we made it this far without one of us keeling over, like at some island waterfall for instance . . . stopping to rest every time we turn around . . . artificial knees . . ." he got on the elevator and made an irritated jab at the top button labeled "Sun Deck," ". . . and then of course my damned breathing!" He was wheezing.

As good fortune would have it, the elevator was empty which meant that he could cool down—he didn't want to be caught off guard again should he run across more of these shipmates overly enthused about his group of old guys. He slowed his breathing to the rhythm of the elevator as it jiggled up two floors. Focusing on the elevator button labeled "Sun Deck" seemed to brighten his spirits—scripted in lively yellow and orange with a little sun painted on the side, the button stood out from the others, like an enticement. "Well, what the heck, I'm going to get those pictures I was after," he said as if someone was standing there with him. Then as he stepped out of the elevator, he added in that pretend drawl again, "*Ya'll* just wait and see!" He smiled to himself.

It was Russ's inquisitive nature that taught him most of what he knew in life, always a zest for learning something new, looking for possibilities, an eye for detail, and just plain simple observation. That's why he wanted to walk every deck and see the workings of a great ship such as this *Fantasy* that brought him back so many years ago to the *Queen Mary* carrying troops overseas. So now, finally here on the top deck where in fact as he looked around and saw a still-higher vantage point, he thought, "Heck, I've come this far, I must as well check that out too, and tell the guys I got to the highest place on this darned ship." What got his attention was a narrow flight of stairs with a gate at the bottom and a sign "European Sun Pool," and even though his legs were tired and achy and he really needed a place to sit, his curiosity won out again. He opened the gate and climbed the stairs.

But Russ wasn't prepared for what happened next. What he was about to see wasn't included anywhere in the cruise literature and for that matter was so out of the realm of his world that it could only be categorized as one those lifetime experiences credited to an inquisitive nature. The discovery was not unlike his experiences stumbling upon, say, deer or wild turkeys or morel mushrooms or wild chestnuts, or even relic arrowheads when poking around in the woods, in that it was a surprise find—like an award of sorts for persistence and keeping one's eyes open. But *this* discovery left him speechless, light-headed, and even questioning his own mental state. Quite unlike his finds out in the wild, grounded in the natural order of things, this discovery was without natural order whatsoever. Later, he would reason that surely it was the effect of a balmy tropical breeze on a luxurious boat that caused this odd behavior. *That's* what swayed some otherwise normal women to throw all caution aside and *shed their shirts*! What other reason could there be for half naked women to display their wares in broad daylight? "European Sun Pool," as that name now flashed before his eyes in a mental hurried retracing of just where he made a wrong turn and why he was now gawking at bare breasts, apparently was a nice way of saying "topless area." "Ah huh," he said under his breath as he edged as close to the outer railing as he could manage and held on tight to steady himself . . . "European . . ."

Breasts of all sizes seemed to be gazing back at him—tanned, glistening with oil and sparkling with the sun's rays hitting the pool on that small deck enclosure. Russ blinked and adjusted his glasses. Yes, it was true. Ever so quietly, he tried to clear the catch in his throat. A couple of lethargic heads from the deck chairs lifted to check on the strange newcomer, their large round sunglasses catching the reflections too like the glistening breasts. He acknowledged them by a nod and a feeble, "Hello . . . ah, sorry . . ." and a gulp—but, except for a couple of coy grins, the faces were vacant and disappeared again under their hats. Russ fumbled with his camera as if the Instamatic Kodak required a special setting, then tucked it in his shirt pocket and pretended to busy himself by searching for something important, possibly something he forgot that might explain why he must suddenly leave only a second after arriving. Mixed in the loose change in his pants pocket he felt the room key, a welcome reminder of a safer place, and he held it tightly as if a rudder as he turned to go back down the steps. "Watch your step, sir." A bleached-blond, over-weight woman wrapped in a large white terry towel was on her way up so that he had to turn and lean into the railing as she squeezed by. He tipped his cap and smiled, "Yes, miss, these steps sure are risky."

Once down the steps and out the gate, he quickened his pace to a modified skip/two-step kind of stride, making his way back to the elevators. He tapped his foot and whistled his soft whistle while biding time as he rode the elevator down the ten decks to deck Riviera, and then hurried almost at a dead run through the long corridors back to R-127. Gasping for air again, he fumbled with the key in the lock, his fingers shaking. Finally, a *click*. He swung open the door as if to break-in. There was Elmer sitting on one of the plastic chairs putting on his shoes, with Wheel of Fortune blaring from the television. Russ hurried to the other chair to catch his breath. His eyes were cart wheeling.

"Son of a gun, Elmer, you really missed it this time!"

"Oh you're back, Russel." He was groggy. "Bursting in the door like that could have really scared someone, you know—but I heard you fumbling with the key." He chuckled and continued lacing his shoe. "Missed what? A jackpot at the slot machines? An afternoon show? Something new to eat? I bet that's it . . ." He put his foot down and rested his hands on his knees as he looked over at Russ for the answer.

"Oh, hell no! You wouldn't guess it in a million years, so I might as well tell you—it was one of those, how do you say, *topless* places— a little pool, way the hell on the highest deck. I just walked up some stairs—no one told me *not* to—and there were gals half naked. Half naked, Elmer!" Russ was breathing fast with his hands on his hips.

Elmer blinked and his mouth dropped open.

"They were all laying there out in the open in plain sight. Hell, what was I supposed to do, Elmer? All I was doing was looking for a high spot on the boat to get some last pictures—you know . . . use up the gol' darned film! But I high-tailed it out of there, that's for damned sure! You'd think security would be posted there, someone to check on who goes up there, but no—a guy can just walk right up there, minding his own business, and there you have it—a bunch of half-naked women. Some pretty busty ones too!" Except for the rattling in his lungs, Russ could have stepped in as a boy at a newsstand with the latest edition. He took a couple of long, deep breaths as he shoved his cap back to wipe the sweat from his forehead.

Now Elmer's small eyes were as wide as they could be as he sat there at attention with both hands on his knees, with one shoe on and one shoe off. His voice was crackly at getting out some words. "For heaven's sake, Russel, slow down. Now, tell me: Is that so? Are you sure?" He looked directly into Russ's face for any giveaway whatsoever that this was a prank, even knowing full well that Russ wasn't one for pranks and certainly this was not Russ's type of joke. He waited for a clue.

"Elmer! Do you think I'd make up something like that? Of course that's so! And I definitely was there! It's not exactly something a guy can prove with a picture . . ." He was wringing his hands.

Still processing the juicy news, Elmer looked puzzled. "Well, sorry for doubting you, Russel, but you have to realize that this is *not* the sort of thing people tell you when they go on these cruises. It's always the eats and the shows and the island tours—but nothing, nothing whatsoever, about topless women!" Elmer shook his head in disbelief. Then, slowly a wry smile formed. With a slap to his knee, he let out a howl that startled Russ. "Woweeee, Russel! You hit the jackpot! And golly, here I was taking a nap!" He leaned back in the plastic chair with both hands holding his head. His hearty giggles filled the room like champagne bubbles just uncorked.

Russ stood up with hands on his hips, now amused by his friend's antics, half-dressed body, and silly laugh. "Well, see there— you do believe me. It's the honest to goodness truth. And here you were taking a nap!"

Elmer stopped long enough to gasp, "Tell me again, Russel, how did this all happen?"

So Russ launched into a re-telling of the event but this time the embellished version, beginning with the southern lady and her red lips and ending with the narrow escape past the blond heavy-set woman in the terry towel.

That chance occurrence, as told and re-told so many times in the next two days, served as high-octane fuel for the four men who for the remainder of their trip seemed to navigate the *Fantasy* with a certain ease and even flair, their testosterone levels up a notch. With lighter steps and broader smiles, they held their heads high with all the attention from their adoring shipmates, even if it meant that they stuck out as really old men. Like a badge of honor among themselves, a fraternity for old men, they knew this dark secret of the *Fantasy*. They were in tune for the unexpected on the "fun ship." And as they donned their suits and ties for the captain's dinner, each, with thoughts of his own maleness, reminisced to more youthful care-free days of romance.

On the night before their departure home, Russ laid wide awake in his top bunk with hands folded across his chest, staring at the dark ceiling as he heard snores and slow, heavy breathing from the others. His thoughts had turned to Rich, back home. Russ knew all too well the persistent evils of cancer. "I sure have stories to tell you, Rich . . ." he murmured as he closed his eyes. Then the images shifted to 1944 on the *Queen Mary* . . . and his GI bunkmates . . ."

CHAPTER 13
SO LONG

Rich died that May, three months to the day after the four returned from the *Fantasy*. Russ stopped by every day, no-fail, to visit, always timing the visit after he finished his bookwork at the Texaco station, after his deposit at the bank, and after a cup of coffee at the pool hall. That's when he picked up two of Shelly's fresh-made cinnamon rolls to-go. That was on weekdays. On weekends with the bank and pool hall closed, he did his book work as usual and then picked up two packaged cinnamon rolls from the display at the gas station. Either way, he had a cinnamon roll for Rich when he arrived five to ten minutes before or after ten o'clock. Russ would knock twice on Rich's back door and then let himself in and then forty or forty-five minutes later he would let himself out. Rich liked to tell others, "Russ knows when to visit and when to go."

For the first few weeks, Rich would be in his recliner in front of the television, dressed and covered with an afghan. When he heard the familiar two knocks and the door open and close, he would holler back towards the kitchen, "Best of the morning to you, Russel! What's a busy young fella like you doing here today?" and he'd wait for Russ to holler back on cue, "Just here to chew the fat for a couple minutes with an old Dane." Russ then would join him in the living room, serving up coffee and the cinnamon rolls. Always they talked first about the weather, then the latest news of the Gang and who might or might not have been in the pool hall or on Vernon Avenue that morning, and then on any number of topics including past and present planting seasons. Russ covered it all in detail.

In the last few weeks, Rich was confined to bed. First it was his regular bed, and then by order of the doctor, a high, oversized one that adjusted up and down, just like in a hospital. A nurse was with him around the clock. Russ did most of the talking from then on, except for an occasional whispered comment from Rich. His eyes were closed much of the time, and when open, had an unusual distant stare in a darker shade of blue.

Still, Russ carried on the conversation not much different than if the two had been playing cards at the pool hall or making a batch of potato pancakes in Russ's kitchen. "Say, did you hear why Ole left the Lutheran Church?" he'd tease with the retelling of one of Rich's old jokes. Or, "That week on the *Fantasy* ship . . ." he'd start off in a string of stories about the bunk beds, the loud toilet, and the topless women. Then Rich would please Russ with a grin. And though not one suited to sit and read, Russ went word-by-word through Rich's mail, the weekly *Morgan Messenger*, and even the fliers with ads on bargains at the Holiday Station in Redwood Falls or the Supermart in New Ulm. Sometimes he filled the silence with just his soft whistle. In those last weeks, Rich's cinnamon roll lay untouched on the bed stand.

One day about a week before Rich's health took this last bad turn, when he was still in his recliner but noticeably growing weaker every day, Russ let his guard down and broke all the rules for visiting the dying. He was irritated at life in general.

"I know we talked about this before, Rich, but . . . what the hell am I supposed to do? Keep driving these guys around?" This he blurted out as he finished his telling of the Gang's recent trip to the Red Wing power plant when the topic on the way home turned to the high price of gas. Even with that fact fresh in their minds, when

Russ did pull up to the gas pump, the others made no effort whatsoever to dig into their own pockets. "Do you think they'd pay for gas once in a while? Hell no! And I'm the one planning all these tours. Hell, we see everything there is to see! We go places!"

Startled at this unusual outburst, Rich just peered over his glasses and waited.

"If *I* don't call, they call *me* and say, 'Hey, Russel, when are you coming to pick me up?'" Russ imitated a phone call as he paced the large braided rug in front of the television. "They can't cook. You remember, Rich, how the two of us could put a meal together? What's so hard about that? Hell, I've never even set foot in Wilbur's house or Hubert's house for that matter." Russ hesitated as he mulled over his facts. "Although, I have say, Hubert *does* pay for my meal every couple of months . . ." Russ resumed his pacing. ". . . and sure as hell not Donnie's house—for goodness sake, he wouldn't know what to do if we all showed up there, and he's the *young* one in the bunch! Rich, do you realize this has been going on for, ah, over seven years?"

Rich closed his eyes and smiled as he nodded, remembering.

Russ tugged at his collar as if to defuse. His pacing slowed. Rich being so quiet in an honorable sort of way threw him off guard, like a conscience. "Now to be fair, Rich, I've got to admit that Elmer does throw in some gas money and his two boys, they'll drive every so often, and, as you know, they have even had us out to their place, which I've got to say was real nice of them. Heck of nice fellas." Realizing that his argument was beginning to sound flimsy, Russ paused

Russ, Wilbur, Donnie, Elmer, and Hubert after touring the power plant.

again to reconsider. Then he had a new twist, "But, but Elmer's getting up there in age. What is he, ninety-three now? What happens when *he* kicks off? What happens then?"

Rich opened his eyes at this break in the discussion and reached for the glass of water on the lamp table next to his recliner. Russ quickly grabbed the glass and turned the straw as he held it up to Rich's mouth. Rich took a long sip, swallowed and motioned with his hand to put the glass back. His voice was weak but his words well thought out. "Well, Russel, like I told you before, it seems to me you just have to think about the alternative—eating *alone*, day after day. We're all going to, ah, as you say, 'kick off' some time. You know that better than most, seeing all that dying in the war. Even *me* . . ." Rich paused with a weak grin and looked up at Russ for a reaction. This was his attempt to lighten the mood a bit and possibly to mention his own failed body. But Russ looked away, more focused it seemed on the window where he could see the first signs of buds on Rich's crabapple tree. Normally a day brightener, he groused as he studied the buds. "And, Russel, don't worry about Elmer—he's tougher than most and probably will outlive us all with that appetite of his." Rich waited again, but Russ was still intent on the window. He crossed his arms and dug back on his heels.

"Say, Russ, about old Elmer's appetite—that reminds me of the Ole and Lena joke when Ole was upstairs in bed dying and he smelled the cookies baking and he snuck down to get one . . ."

"Yeah, yeah . . ." Russ smiled halfheartedly and finished the familiar joke, "Lena says no, he can't have one because she's saving those cookies for the funeral." He turned to see Rich's expectant face about to burst at his favorite joke. He looked like a twelve-year old boy having fun. They laughed.

Russ walked back to the recliner and offered Rich another sip of water. "I guess you're right. Eating alone is no fun . . . no fun at all."

The night before Rich died, his three sons, his daughter and their spouses, all who had been watching over Rich around the clock that weekend, took a long walk just after sunset to clear their senses in the fresh night air. It was an unseasonably warm night for May. Their walk naturally meandered the seven blocks through Vernon Avenue, quiet now with only a couple of cars in front of the VFW, past the library in Vernon Park, and then down the street past St. Michael's Church and finally to Russ's street on the other end of town where they saw a light in the porch. "Good, he's home." One of the shades was halfway up, and they could see him leaning back in his chair. As they walked up the sidewalk to the porch door, they could hear Twins baseball blaring from the radio. They knocked.

"Hello, Russ! Sorry to bother you so late, hope we didn't scare you . . ."

"Gosh, no," Russ tried not to act startled as he looked out in the dark, ". . . oh, *Rich's* kids . . . for gosh sake, come on in. Come on in. Here, let me turn this radio down a bit. Twins are way ahead anyway." He turned down the volume and adjusted his hearing aid. "I didn't see any car lights so, yeah, guess you surprised me a little." He looked out towards the street.

"No, Russ, we just decided to take a little walk. Feels good in the night air. Wanted to see if we could find your house anyway. Had a little argument on which street you're on—then saw you sitting here in the porch." Rich's sons resembled him, but this older one who still farmed in the area even sounded like Rich, and he had the same smile.

"Well the weather tonight is perfect for a walk, that's for sure. Doesn't take much to walk all the streets of Morgan, does it?" Russ always liked to promote the advantages of a small community, but then realized the group probably had more on their minds than an evening walk across town. They looked tired. "Say, how's Rich doing? You know, this morning he even tried to joke a little with me, although with my darned hearing and him talking just in a whisper, I didn't make it all out. I laughed anyway, and he liked that. Sure is a heck of a thing to see him like this."

"Russ, that's just it. The nurse tells us that he's probably not going to make it much longer, just a matter of days probably, but no one knows for sure, of course. You understand. What we really want to know, Russ—well, of course we're thinking about the funeral, you know, planning it all out." The son cleared his throat. "Well, Russ, what we want is for you to say a few words—we'd like you do the eulogy." He kept his eyes steady on Russ as he stammered, and Russ noticed tears held back as the words came out. The others with sad smiles nodded, "Yes, yes," in encouragement. The daughter patted Russ on the shoulder as she wiped away a tear. "It would mean the world to Dad—you and he had something special. And he always told us about what the Gang was doing. He was very proud of you guys."

Russ looked at her and was struck with those familiar, blue, Danish eyes. Then he looked around the group of expectant, tired faces. He jiggled the coins in his pocket, thinking. "Ah, well, I'll tell you right away, I'm not much for public speaking, that's for darned sure, so if you're looking for perfect sounding words and all, well, I'm not it . . ." He hesitated and looked at each of their faces again for any change of mind. ". . . but if it's just a few words about Rich and the Gang . . . if that's what you want, I guess I can't argue." He stood a little taller with his feet planted, now with his commitment to the honor of it all. "Rich has been a very, very good friend." Not much for emotions himself, still, he felt a slight lump in his throat with those words. So he swallowed to ease that uneasiness, firm in his simple faith that life would get better again—all he needed to do was wait and watch. But he wasn't so sure what these kids thought about simple faith—kids pretty much like his own, as far as he could tell—so he didn't want them going out the door just yet with those long faces. He wanted to share some stories. "Here, I'll get some more chairs, and we can talk about it. I could use some company anyway."

For the next hour they cried and laughed and drank coffee, all huddled on that small porch with Twins baseball faint in the background. Russ could almost sense Rich there with them, as if he had just stepped out to pour himself some more coffee. "Hey, Richard," Russ felt the urge to yell out, "get back in here—your kids are here, and we're talking about our Gang." Russ smiled to himself, imagining this. And as they were ready to leave, he sensed Rich's eagerness to leave too, to get to bed at a decent hour.

"Sure. I'll be by at my usual time in the morning—probably I'll see you all again then?" He was holding the door open as they walked out.

"Yes, we'll see you in the morning, Russ. And thanks again for this very special time." They waved. "Have a good night."

"You too. Ah, huh." Russ let the door close but then in a hurry opened it again, yelling after them, "Oh, and you can tell Rich when you get back there that the Twins won. Just heard the announcer, 10 to 2. He'll like that. Good-night, now." Russ locked the door, turned off the light and radio, then stopped to watch out the window as the group rounded the end of the block by the street light—"Nice bunch of kids, Rich," he said and then continued on into the house.

Russ stopped by as usual that next morning and was happy and hopeful again to see that Rich was having one of his good days. He opened his eyes, smiled, and even motioned for Russ to come closer to tell him, "good season," after Russ talked at length about the baseball game. And when Russ was ready to leave, Rich reached for Russ's hand to pull him close, then squeezed Russ's hand hard and whispered, "So long, Russel."

"Yeah, so long, Rich. I'll see you tomorrow, same time as usual."

It was that afternoon when Russ was contemplating a nibble on his line just after a perfect cast to his lucky fishing spot—two-thirds across the river and slightly downstream from the boat landing—when Rich took his last breath. Russ waited with his usual patience for that second nibble, picturing the walleye ten feet or so down in the murky river water sizing up the bait, making a quick turn and then grabbing it for good. Russ set the hook and reeled, exhilarated as he pulled in a three-pound walleye. "Well, I'll be darned! And with the river this high!" He slipped his cap back and scratched his head in wonder. With his expectations set low for early spring fishing after the thaw and high waters, Russ considered the catch highly unusual. He had come to the river this afternoon as more of a peace-finding expedition for he knew that an afternoon in the valley had never failed to lift his spirits. A few casts in the river, watching it flow gently by, that's all he intended to sooth his soul today. So after a couple more casts with no further action, he was content to pack up his gear and head for home, considering himself very lucky to have a nice-sized walleye in the trunk of his car. He turned on the radio, pleased to tune in the Twins afternoon game on his ride home. He rolled down his window for more of that fresh spring air, picking up speed and talking to himself with a smile, "Soon as I get home, I'll call and get a hold of one of Rich's kids to see how Rich is doing—they can tell him I'll be bringing over some walleye. He'll like that."

Three days later, an early Thursday morning, Russ was muttering in front of his closet as he pulled out his suit: "Suits are good for only three things—weddings, cruises, and funerals." Then, checking his watch, he stopped himself. "Hell, it's too early to be dressed in this get-up—I've got a couple of hours yet." He tossed the suit on the bed and marched back to his recliner in the living room. He pulled out the small notebook from his shirt pocket and began to jot down thoughts that came easily now after a sleepless night rehearsing. Then, setting the notebook aside and adjusting the chair to a full recline, he rested his head back and closed his eyes. "Sure as hell don't want to be long-winded, Rich—you remember how we talked about those damned, long-winded preachers," he worried out loud just before he dozed off.

The Methodist Church was familiar to Russ because that's where he was raised as a child. But even more than that, the church was familiar because every winter for as long as he could remember the Methodist Men's Group sponsored a chow mein supper in the basement. The sanctuary was used as a coat room for all of the winter coats that were tossed on the pews while families attended the supper downstairs. Later, as the parents lingered over their meals and conversations, the children raced up and down the sanctuary aisles. But today, the sanctuary had a stately, solemn feel about it, except for the occasional mistake by the organist as she played variations of How Great Thou Art on the full-sized electric Hammond situated right there in front for all to watch.

The Gang filed in and sat in the reserved row directly behind Rich's family. Each with a red carnation in his lapel, they were honorary pallbearers—Wilbur, Donnie, Hubert, Elmer, and then Russ next to the aisle.

The sanctuary was crowded. People shuffled and moved over in the pews to make more room, and finally the ushers brought in folding chairs to add a row in the back. The weather was sunny and warm so one of the ushers began opening some of the windows, bringing in the fresh spring air loaded with smells of lilacs and crab apple blossoms.

After the procession and four stanzas of "Just as I Am," the preacher, read a verse from *John*, spoke about life's ups and downs and the life hereafter, and then nodded to Russ as a cue. Russ walked up to the lectern and with a shaky hand pulled out the slip of paper from his shirt pocket. He adjusted his bifocals to see better the scribbled, sparse notes that now he wished were bigger and with full sentences: "Hotdish—Widowers—Cooking Meals Together—Restaurants—Side Trips—Twins Baseball—Years of Friendship—Rich's Jokes." He cleared his throat and looked up out at the crowd of expectant faces. Past the five pews of the Frederiksen family, he saw all the familiar faces from town—members of the Morgan Elevator Board and their wives, bank employees, Rich's neighbors, the town cop, the barber, the regulars from the pool hall, and towards the back he even recognized a couple of waitresses from the Country Kitchen in Redwood Falls. Seeing all these faces now, gathered here at this church to remember one of their own, he realized that all they really wanted was a word of hope, nothing more. He stood a little taller, planted his feet, and tucked the notes back in his pocket.

"Living all my life here in Morgan," he began, "I didn't even become acquainted with Richard Frederiksen until seven years ago. That's when my wife, Lorraine, died. It might sound a little odd to some of you, but it was a hotdish that got us together . . ." This was a story the townspeople knew by bits and pieces picked up here and there over the past seven years, at the pool hall, the bank, even the ladies church circle groups where the latest news about the Gang filtered into their designated minutes for fellowship. Now they were glued to Russ's words. For ten minutes he spoke, going even beyond his notes into some examples of Rich's cooking achievements, including his famous baked beans and roasts. "Yes, sir, Rich could cook." Russ paused, looking from one side of the sanctuary to the other, hoping to drive home his next point. ". . . *but more than that*, he loved to be around people. That's probably what mattered most to him. Rich didn't care if we had home-cooked meals or restaurant food—he was happy just to be around people. Guess that's why we're all here." Russ returned to his seat.

The church was silent. Then, as if next on the order of service, a robin chirped a tune outside the front window, causing more than a few to turn and nod with reverent smiles. As the organist shuffled the pages to the hymnal, some sniffled and coughed, and a man near the front loudly blew his nose. Peering down through her bifocals, the organist finally settled on a page, secured it with an oversize clip, and with head back and chin up, she began a rousing introduction to "Amazing Grace."

Several from the ladies aide group in the back row tip-toed out during the hymn in their hurry to get downstairs to prepare for the lunch following the interment. Though not a Methodist, Agnes Ziegenhagen sat with them because she always donated a cake or hotdish for funerals and liked to help out wherever needed—it was her nature. "I'll be down in just a few minutes, Merna," she whispered, not taking her eyes off the row of honorary pallbearers. "I'd like to stay until the end of the service."

Chapter 14
Jams and Pickles

The knock at the door came just as Oprah was interviewing a woman from the audience about inappropriate behavior at the workplace. A recent court case had just awarded several women employees at a meatpacking plant in Illinois a handsome settlement for what they called sexual harassment, a new term for Russ and one that was coming up a lot in the news lately. He tuned into *Oprah* most afternoons because, for one thing, it opened up a world of women's topics he never had imagined or considered important, and he was intrigued by all the fuss. The other thing was Oprah sure knew how to entertain, especially for a black gal.

"Yeah, just a minute," he hollered as he got up from his recliner and headed to the back entry, a little stiff from his gardening that afternoon. He looked out the small window of the door and saw Agnes Ziegenhagen, a woman he knew through the years as Walter Ziegenhagen's widow and before that Henry Grabow's widow. She was a member of the "other" Lutheran church in Morgan, the stricter Missouri synod Zion Lutheran. After raising her family on the farm and losing her second husband, she moved into town and now had a house just a block from the Zion church. Both the Ziegenhagens and the Grabows had been customers of Albrecht's Fairway over the years, though not the big, steady customers that Russ would normally become more acquainted with to say more than a casual greeting. She was waiting now with her arms wrapped around herself holding her coat tightly, and when she noticed his face in the window, she beamed. He opened the door. "Well, hello there, Agnes. You're here with a payment for Beneficial, I bet."

She was bundled up with extra clothes, it seemed to Russ, for so early in the fall. On the other hand, the wind had been whipping up today, drier and cooler after the days of Indian summer, so a coat wouldn't be out of the question. Now as a gust swirled the dry, colorful leaves on the back steps where she stood, the wind seemed playful. Agnes was heavy-set, to Russ's standards, but well-proportioned and sturdy for a woman in her eighties. The one thing Russ knew for sure was that she was all German from that thick brogue of hers that had remained the same over the years as though she just stepped off the boat. A red scarf was tied loosely over her head with wisps of white hair escaping around her wide face. Her smile showed off teeth as white as her hair and, Russ noticed too, as white as the fluffy clouds in the background of the bright fall sky as she stood there on his steps.

"Come in, come in. It's a little chilly out there with the way that wind is gusting. Sure is a swell fall day though with that bright sunshine." He held the door open wide while she stepped inside, struggling to hold her coat close to her.

"Yeah, Russel, it sure is a beautiful day." She enunciated "Russel" like a drill sergeant, reminding him of his German grandmother straight from the old country, and it tickled him enough to make him grin. She stepped a bit closer to him, closer than he was used to, and looked him straight in the eye as if to share a secret. "I know how you like da outdoors, Russel. Me too! Even on a day like dis with all the vind—I like it!" Her brusque pronunciation and serious eyes belied the flirting smile forming on her rosy lips. Her enthusiasm for the topic seemed as fresh as the air outside, which is likely why Russ took a big breath to soak it all in.

"Whew! You're absolutely right, Agnes. Perfect weather to be outdoors. That's for sure." He edged back a step to a more comfortable distance and planted both feet with his arms folded across his chest. "I just came in from the garden after digging spuds all afternoon—four bushel baskets, that's what I got, all loaded in the root cellar. That was a hundred hills I planted this year. Boy, that's a good feeling! Heck of a lot of work, but couldn't ask for a better day to do it!" Appropriately distanced now, he found himself enjoying this unexpected moment of having an attentive listener.

"My heavens, Russel—you are in very fine shape to keep up a garden *dat* size. I always said dat gardening keeps a person strong, yah. And you, Russel—you're always on da go—at least dat's vhat I hear. Dat's why you're so . . . so trim. Don't you tink? Not fat, like some." She eyed him up and down which seemed to trigger a nervous tapping with his foot.

"Yeah, well, I probably got that from my dad who never had a problem with weight. My mother either. Both real slender." Russ didn't see any sense talking any more about weight since he was sure that Agnes outweighed him by quite a few pounds. "Yup, well anyway, I've got to say, Ages, you are really quick paying Beneficial this time—think I sent the notification on Reynold Severson just yesterday." He checked his watch. "Ah huh, just yesterday . . ."

Agnes's eyes turned sad, and she gave a heavy sigh. "Oh, Russel. Isn't it just awful how Reynold suffered?" She shook her head in what some might consider was an overly dramatic display of concern, although Russ knew enough about some of her own tough times to know that the display was genuine. "And now Emma is left with da fall harvesting. It's just good dat her boys live nearby to help. I just vonder if she'll stay on da farm. Da funeral, I heard, is Vednesday, at St. Michael's, ah huh. I'm going to take a hotdish over tomorrow so Emma has plenty to feed her houseful." She sighed again and dropped her eyes, swaying her head to those thoughts as she still clutched her middle. "Hmm." That's when she noticed that Russ was still tapping his foot. Her face brightened, and she looked up. She couldn't help but be amused at his nervous energy, and that brought her back into focus for her original purpose. "Yeah, Russel, I got your card today so tought I might as vell drive it over—dat way you have it!" Her smile was so warm and her expression so honest that even Russ was convinced that he needed the four-dollar payment at that very moment.

"Oh! And Russel . . . vait a minute . . ." Realizing she couldn't hand over the payment until she freed her hands from a more important delivery, with special care she pulled back the side of her coat. There, half hidden in the layers of her sweater and coat, Russ saw three small Mason jars that she was holding fast against her blouse. "I brought you someting else, Russel, besides the payment . . . but I didn't tink you vould vant your neighbors to see. You know how people talk . . ."

Russ could manage only a quizzical nod.

With the loving care of an artisan unveiling her works, she displayed each jar on the nearby table. "One of my sweet pickles and two of my raspberry jam!" She took a step back to admire. "I just put dem up a couple weeks ago and tought you could use some home cooking—living here by yourself, you know." She adjusted one of the jars to line up with the others.

Glistening in the ray of sun from the window, the jars were picture-perfect really, like in a glossy magazine on country living. The rich fall colors of green and raspberry-red were sumptuous and bold through the thick glass, with the shiny gold rings and lids accenting the seal of home goodness. A handwritten label on each jar confirmed it: "9/15/92" with a curlicue "Agnes" in red marker.

Russ stopped his toe tapping and adjusted his glasses. "Well! Ah, this looks like . . . like county fair material, it seems to me! No, no, I take that back—*state* fair material." He choked a laugh. "My gosh, Agnes, don't you think those should be in a contest somewhere? At least you should save these for your company!" Russ twirled one of the jars, hoping more words would come to him.

Agnes blushed. "No, no, Russel, dese are for *you*. I vant you to have dem. Besides . . ." she paused and caught herself batting her eyes, "dere's plenty more vere dese came from!" Not really intending to end with such a zinger, yet feeling fairly comfortable about it now that it was out, she had to giggle.

At this, Russ was convinced just about one-hundred percent that she might be suggesting more than just canning from her garden. The full dynamics of the situation now confirmed the uneasiness he had from the very start: That Agnes Ziegenhagen, standing here at his doorway and smelling faintly of perfume and the October wind that still hung to her clothes, was a woman alone. She had buried two husbands in her lifetime and now here she was in his house bringing him presents! He was out of words.

"Ah, huh, *state* fair material . . ." He continued to busy himself twirling the jars and as he did so, realized that they were still warm from her body. He put his hands in his pockets.

Agnes cleared her throat to stifle her giggles and began fishing in her coat pocket. She brought out folded dollar bills. "Oh, and here, Russel, this is my Beneficial payment for Reynold, four dollars." She handed over the dollar bills and seemed to make a point of pressing them into his hand. Her hands, he couldn't help but notice, were strong and steady, showing years of hard work, but somehow off-limits with fingernails painted a bright pink.

Glad to focus on the four dollar bills instead, he held them out for a better look, as if these dollar bills were unusual somehow. "Well, your payment is the first I've received on Reynold. Heck, you could get a prize for that too! Yes, Agnes—a prize for that too!"

Her proud smile waited for him to say more, but he was stuck for good, it seemed, and instead resumed his tapping. He looked back at the Mason jars. "And . . . ah . . . well . . . this is real nice, Agnes. Thank you very much! You bet . . . this is real nice, ah huh."

"Yeah, Russel, I tink you *deserve* a little home-cooking. Don't you?" Agnes just couldn't resist fishing for some details.

It was more like stoking the fire, for Russ, who now since Rich was gone had been re-thinking the exact nature of his role with the others in the Gang who weren't exactly the self-starting type. "Ah, well, I don't know about *deserve* but you're sure right, Agnes, that I don't get much home cooking these days—that is, except when I get a notion to do it myself." Russ stopped tapping his foot. He folded his arm across his chest, resting his chin in his hand, as if to end the topic there.

"And da odders? Do dey cook?"

Russ fidgeted with his chin. "The guys, well . . . they *don't* cook, so we go to restaurants." He looked at her with a leery eye before saying more. "Heck, they don't even like to drive, so I pick them up and we go—make a night out of it. We just head out of town." He paused, again leery.

Agnes's gentle smile waited for more.

"But, you know, I haven't even seen the inside of their houses after all these years. Shoot, they just wait for someone to plan it for them, like I'm the only one with a car. Well, I'm the only *driver*, that's for sure. Well, of course, Rich, when he was around, he liked to cook and we'd get a meal going, the two of us. We'd cook for the whole bunch! Sure as heck miss that guy. And well, Elmer's boys every so often have us out for a real nice meal—roast beef, the works. Do you realize that Elmer is pretty near ninety-five now?" Russ felt like a runaway train with his words spilling out.

Agnes just nodded with a look of concern. It was then that Russ realized how quiet she had been, letting him spout off, and in some detail too—exactly *not* what he had intended. Agnes, he knew, was known for staying current on *all* aspects of the Morgan community, and the Gang had enough gossip going around as it was. "Damn it," he told himself. Then, figuring he could smooth it out with a snappy ending and send her on her way, he eased toward the door as he continued, ". . . but, you're absolutely right about that, Agnes—I don't get much home-cooking. And these jams and pickles just fit the bill!" With an exaggerated grin, he put his hand on the doorknob, which he knew was always a good signal for guests that overstay their visit. "Thank you very much, Agnes. I'm sure I'll enjoy these!" He opened the door.

Agnes seemed cemented to the linoleum. "You are very velcome, Russel. The raspberries are from—"

"Oh, and I'll record your payment on Reynold right away. I believe you're up to date as usual." He stuffed the dollar bills in his shirt pocket and moved around her slightly to push open the screen door. He looked up at the sky to confirm that the sun and fluffy clouds were still there while he shuffled Agnes along with his out-stretched arm. "Yeah, you bet, it's a nice day out there . . . "And this wind is sure bringing the leaves down. You know, fall is my favorite time of the year, that's for sure."

"*Me too*, Russel!" Agnes burst out with those words like a school girl overly excited to bond. She had stopped halfway out the door to look Russ straight in the eye with this development. "And dat's vhen da *fish* start biting again!"

With her stopping like that and Russ so close at her heels, he couldn't keep from bumping into her, and now her face was just inches from his. "Oops." He stepped back on the threshold, still holding the door open and still holding his breath. "Yeah, Agnes— fall is the best time to fish, that's for sure."

This sort of impromptu contact felt just right to Agnes and caused a certain flush to her face. She giggled. "Russel, you probably don't know just *how much* I like to fish, *especially* at da river. I could fish for *hours* on a day like dis!" She bit her lip to keep from saying more, knowing full well that she would pick up on this topic another time soon, a time when Russ wouldn't be squirming in his shoes like she sensed today.

In his most unimpressed, matter-of-fact voice, Russ replied, "Well, good. I've heard that a lot of women really enjoy it. No reason why not to . . . no reason at all." He was glad at least to keep his end of the conversation on the up and up, although he was a bit distracted at the girlish flush in her cheeks—he hoped the distraction didn't show.

The wind gusted and swirled some leaves through the doorway, and even Russ had to laugh as he tried to keep the leaves from blowing in. "Guess I'd better close this door or I'll have a mess inside," he said.

Agnes took the hint. "Vell, den, Russel . . ." she held the end of his name like a note holding a full count, then continued in sing-song. ". . . I'll be on my vay now. Be sure to let me know how you like dose pickles and jams." I can bring over some more . . ." With her hand on the railing, she smiled up at the sky with eyes closed, and she drew in a big breath. "Yeah, vhat a beautiful day, Russel!" As she went down the steps, she shrugged off her coat. "My goodness, a sweater is all I need on such a nice afternoon." She turned and waved as she walked to her car, with leaves swirling around her feet. Her red scarf seemed to be waving too. "You have a nice afternoon, Russel!"

Still holding the door open, Russ took a deep breath too, bit his lip to reconsider saying any more that might just lead to trouble. But he ignored that prompt and called out after her anyway, "Oh, and for me, fishing is one of those things that can make a headache go away. That's how much I like it. And that's no kidding."

She smiled and got in her car.

It was only two days later when a daughter called at her usual time on Sunday. To Russ it could have been forever with news like this bottled up, like the steam from the pan of boiling spuds he was watching on the stove that afternoon. He didn't have a soul in town to trust with this bit of information, if in fact it was information even worth mentioning. Everyone in town was connected to everyone else, and eventually one of the guys would find out—and by then, it likely would be embellished. News like this could keep the lips flapping in the pool hall and in churches for months. This was what had been on his mind.

So, keeping it all to himself, with his mind doing twists and turns of every detail, he even wondered if he might have imagined the whole thing—that his morning brandy got the better of him or even that he had one of those little strokes he'd been hearing about on the new WCCO radio show, senior health news. "No," he reasoned as he half-dozed in front of the television later that Sunday evening, "I've got the pickles and jam to prove it!" Just to double-check, he got up from his recliner and peeked around the corner into the kitchen to see the three jars still lined up on his counter.

The phone finally rang about mid-way through *The Golden Girls*. The conversation with the daughter had run its course with the usual exchange of news since last Sunday's call—the weather, the television line-up, and the latest news about the Gang—when Russ eased into the hot topic. "Oh, yeah . . ." he started out and stopped to clear his throat as a technique for the build-up, ". . . I had a very interesting visitor the other day, someone you'd never guess . . ." He waited, tapping his fingers on the armrest, and eyes glazed at Bea Arthur on the television.

"Really? Who?"

"A gal, err, a woman, I should say." He waited again.

"Who, Dad? Who?"

"Well, maybe you never knew of her—I think her kids were a couple of grades ahead of you—but it was . . . ah . . . Agnes Ziegen-hagen!" The name spilled out like an eager answer in class.

Her voice trailed. "Agnes Ziegenhagen . . . ? Ah, gosh Dad, I'm not sure who that is . . ."

"Oh, for heaven's sake! *You* know, she was married for years to Henry Grabow and lived on that farm east of town. Then after he died, she married Walter Ziegenhagen, moved to town, and now *he's* gone. She's real German—I mean, she still talks that way. Says 'dis' and 'dat,' you know, real German." Losing his momentum with the story, Russ felt his blood pressure take a turn up.

"Hm, I'm not sure *who* that is."

"Well, *anyway* . . ." Russ took a slow breath. ". . . she came to the door the other day with the Beneficial payment. That, of course, isn't unusual—it's pretty common that folks just stop by to drop off their payment instead of mailing it, you know, just to stop and chew the fat. But *she* has never stopped by before, always mailed the payment."

"Ah, huh . . ."

"Well, that's not all of it—just let me finish." Russ readjusted in the recliner. "She brought me some jars of her pickles and jams too. Real nice looking stuff, but gol darn, here she was pulling out all these jars from her coat. You see, she had them hidden in her coat so the neighbors wouldn't know! That's what she said! That's the honest to goodness truth!"

"No. You mean it?"

"That's absolutely right. I kind of thought something looked different with her coat all bunched up around her middle but didn't say anything, of course. She's not exactly a skinny person. Then, here she brings out these jars—hell of a predicament, I'll tell you that much!" Russ slapped the armrest and sat up a little straighter with a grin like he just delivered a punch line.

"Wow, Dad! Now let me get this straight—you say she's *not* married?"

"That's right, *not* married. Her last husband, Walter, must have died, oh, probably it was last winter. Heart attack, I think."

"Well . . . then, all I can say is: She's *after* you, Dad! I'll bet you anything! Why else would she . . ."

Russ felt himself about to giggle too, just like his daughter, but thought it best to tamper it a bit and play it down. "Naw, I'm just telling you this because it's a little . . . oh . . . *peculiar,* if you know what I mean. Hiding the stuff like that." Russ pulled his handkerchief from his pocket and wiped the beads of sweat on his forehead.

"How old is she? What does she look like—I mean, is she attractive?" The words tumbled over the phone in a high pitch. This sort of information could be a God-send really for a daughter after years of worry and guilt about how Dad would manage all alone. The old guys for certain had taken care of his social needs these last few years, and she was humbly thankful for those fine men, but a female relationship? Well, that was far down her list of other late-in-life scenarios in such an out-of-the-way place as Morgan.

"Well, she's not a beauty queen, if that's what you mean, but a heck of nice person. Not a spring chicken either, probably as old as I am, that's for darned sure. Yeah, in fact, she might even be . . ."

"That's just fine, Dad! Let's see, so now . . . how can we . . . hmm."

Russ had the sinking feeling he was getting into something over his head.

". . . you need to do something nice for her, really nice. Yes, this is perfect. Hmmm, you could, um, well let's see . . . take something from your garden, you could even invite her over or take her out . . . *yes*, that's it, you could take her out . . . how about that, Dad?. . . take her to . . ."

"*Hold* on just a minute now—I don't have to do anything like that!" he snapped. That sinking feeling apparently was right-on, except now he sensed being *completely* over his head. "Besides, old Agnes knew what she was talking about—the neighbors *would* have a hay-day. I'd be the talk of Morgan. Cripes, I've got plenty going on with the guys, and the town is talking enough about us the way it is. I don't need to figure something like this in too." Russ wished he'd kept his mouth shut. The last time he listened to his daughter, he wound up with a dog that barked nonstop, which almost got him fined by the city. The memory was clear now, and he wasn't about to get talked into another mess.

"*All* I was telling you was that I have this food, so I'd better eat it or find a way to get rid of it, that's all! Hell, I don't even eat sweet pickles! You girls and your mother were the ones who ate those. In fact, *you* can have the pickles!" Russ actually knew that none of what he said followed any logic and that he likely set himself up for exactly this reaction. He felt foolish for even bringing it up and then barking at his daughter when she offered suggestions—so he backed off. "Now, as for the jam, that's okay, I guess—except for those damned seeds. They get in my dentures."

That was all really that Russ could muster for excuses, so when he hung up some ten minutes later, he had promised that at least he would *consider* the possibility of returning the nice gesture. His daughter had high hopes. Beauty queen or not, any eighty-something female with this much self-assurance and fortitude definitely deserved another look. She phoned her sisters.

Meanwhile, Russ pushed the recliner position back and turned the TV up extra loud for the closing scene of *Golden Girls*. Life seemed complicated, made-up or real, and for now, he'd just as soon focus on the made-up. Still, the notion lingered that in the real world his daughters might be critical of a female friend. He had heard stories like that on *Oprah*.

For the next several weeks, Russ busied himself with gardening and fall yard work, his usual bookkeeping tasks and several supper outings with the Gang. He was the driver, of course. One Friday, he even organized a special day-long trip some three hours away across the state to see the latest exhibits at Farm Fest, the annual fall celebration of mid-west farming. Still, each morning he spread a thick layer of raspberry jam on his toast and then carefully chewed, working his way around the seeds. The second jar was almost gone.

Then, on a Sunday late afternoon the phone rang: "Yeah, Russel—isn't anyone going to eat? This is Elmer. Hubert just called me wondering too."

"Oh, hello, Elmer." Russ had a notion that the others would depend on Elmer to finally make a call since Elmer was a bit of an organizer too. Even with his age, ninety-four just last month, he would take on the responsibility of rounding up the guys, if it got down to it. Russ respected that.

"Well, I suppose it's getting about that time again—let's see, it's five o'clock on the nose. Just what do you and Hubert have in mind? It's Sunday night, you know, and most places aren't open." Sounding like this was the furthest thing from his mind when in fact it was such a regular occurrence that the waitress at Country Kitchen could write up the order right this minute as they talked on the phone—calico soup all around on Sunday evenings—still, Russ didn't feel particularly guilty about purposely waiting for the call and now sounding somehow new to the whole idea. He knew he had them over a barrel.

These days it bothered Russ only slightly that no one else would drive—he was resigned to the fact: Hubert and Elmer had given up driving beyond Morgan's city limits. Donnie's car was too small, seating only five, and he'd be all nerves anyway, taking those pills again. And Wilbur, well, Russ would just as soon never ride again with him behind the wheel with those jerky starts and stops and peeling out to turn with no thought whatsoever to what was coming down the road. The last time Wilbur was behind the wheel he almost got them all killed. That's when Irv Johansen's semi full of sweet corn had to swerve on to the gravel shoulder at the last second, nearly sending him into the ditch. Wilbur's excuse later was just that his bifocals needing adjusting. So now, waiting for Elmer's call really served no purpose for Russ, except possibly to test his own resolve that somehow change was in the air.

"How about this, Russel? You pick us up in about, oh, say, twenty minutes, and we just head over to Country Kitchen in Redwood—we know that's open. Some of that calico bean soup sounds pretty good tonight, huh? I'll call Donnie and Wilbur and get right back to you. What do you say, Russel?"

"Hmm, calico soup—well, yeah, that sounds pretty good to me too." Russ hung on the word like he wasn't sure. "Okay then, you call me back so I know who I'm picking up." As if promptness was ever an issue, he warned, "But tell them they'd better be ready!"

"Or what?" Russ thought later, even amused now with his attitude. Over these last years he had become responsible really for these guys, whether he liked it or not. ". . . Better be ready or I'm driving away without them? Hmph, not much of a threat—they're *always* ready."

That night was no different—after a long quiet Sunday afternoon, they were eager to get out of their houses, punctual to say the least, waiting for their ride and watching out the windows long before the Taurus drove up. And certainly Russ in his right mind could have no complaints about the leisurely drive through Minnesota farm country, always so easy on the eyes, and with easy conversation too along the way about crops and weather. Then too, there was the camaraderie of sharing a simple meal with men, alone like himself. He knew of others in town who would give their eye teeth to be included in a group like this. "What the hell—I don't want to bollix this up!" This was his nagging thought as the Taurus headed back to Morgan that fall evening.

Hubert was the last one to be dropped off, in reverse order of the pick-up routine. "Okay, then, Hubert—see you Thursday night for the Methodist chow mein supper. You heard Wilbur say that he'll get the tickets, since it's his church and all—but we'll see if he remembers. Half the time I'm not sure he knows what day it is any more."

"Yeah, okay." Hubert's long legs didn't function well from the position of a car seat so he had to lift each one up and then out of the door. He mumbled something about getting "crippled up." Upright, he steadied himself on the car door for a few seconds and then without saying any more, he ambled off to his house, giving Russ a little back-handed wave to signal it was okay to leave. Russ waited a minute more until Hubert was inside and the yard light was turned off.

Russ shook his head and sighed as he backed out and headed home. He turned to the empty passenger seat and continued with a conversation. "Yeah, don't mention it, Hubert. No trouble at all. Oh, and you say you want to fill the gas tank next time? Well, that would be nice . . ." He smiled, shook his head, and sighed.

Still mulling, he turned onto his street, and it was then that he noticed a particular starkness to his house, there in the middle of the block, as if vacant. "Hmm." Then, realizing he had simply forgotten to leave the light on, he quickly dismissed the dark notion.

Standing on the back steps for a minute before going inside, he gazed up at the stars in the cool darkness. The stars oftentimes set him straight on the order of things. After all, it was a star that night forty-some years ago that told him he would be okay as he hid in a foxhole in Belgium. Satisfied with that memory, he went inside to settle into his recliner and wait for the nine o'clock news. On his way through the kitchen, he couldn't help but notice the empty Mason jars on the counter, sparkling clean now and set out there this morning as a reminder to be returned. "Hmm . . ."

The next four days as Russ went about his usual activities, an idea percolated, as ideas sometimes do, especially for big decisions. Scheduling, that's really all it was—simple scheduling. Nothing complicated about that, he told himself, as he stood at the wall calendar one afternoon. He moved his finger across the days. "Now, if the chow mein supper is Thursday night, the guys won't be calling to go out until Saturday night, leaving Friday clear-sailing, hmm," he said under his breath. But, like any plan to be secret or, at the very least, not to create attention, details were critical. He reviewed and then reviewed again all the contingencies: destination, time, route, and, most important, the likely spot the town cop might park to watch the comings and goings in Morgan that night. "Oh, what the heck, I might as well try," Russ coached himself, as he picked up the phone before leaving to meet the guys at the chow mein supper.

"Yeah, hello, Agnes?"

"Yeah?"

"This is Russ, Russ Albrecht. Just wanted to . . ."

"Oh, *yes*, Russel! How are you?"

Startled by her strong, clear, and what seemed like an overly enthusiastic voice, he held the receiver out so he could adjust his hearing aid. "Oh, fine, just fine . . . um, I just had to adjust, ah . . . well, anyway, just wanted

Agnes Ziegenhagen.

to tell you again thank you very much for the jars you brought over, you know, the jams and pickles?"

"Yeah. Did you . . ."

"Well, I finished up the raspberry this morning. Heck of a good taste!"

Agnes was smiling on the other end with his quickness in getting all that out. She could tell he was nervous. "You know, Russel . . . I have more to give you, *vemember*? I have some chokecherry here, that I just put up today. Do you like chokecherry too, Russel?" Her words were slow and enticing.

"Oh, chokecherry—now that's really my favorite—yeah, grew up eating that! And that doesn't have the seeds so it works a little better, you know, with these choppers of mine." Not really intending to bring that up, Russ bit his lip, waiting for her reaction.

"Oh, Russel, you should have told me dat seeds are a problem, you poor ting. Dis chokecherry should be just perfect den!"

He smiled. No more seeds. "Well, more of that jam would be just fine, no hurry though. But, um . . . say, I was wondering too if maybe I could buy you . . . oh, how about supper? Say tomorrow night? That would be Friday." He traced his fingers across the calendar again. "Hmm, that's right, isn't it? Today is Thursday . . . so yes, Friday. Friday for supper." Just to pay you back, you know." He clenched his jaw and waited again.

What he couldn't see, of course, was Agnes beaming like a schoolgirl as she stood with the phone in one hand and her other hand on her chest as though holding her heart to count the beats. Standing there at her kitchen window, with her mind racing her eyes locked outside on the brilliant golden-red leaves still hanging on the maple tree in her front yard. She was astounded how precisely the leaves caught the sun at this much anticipated moment, like prisms. She took a deep breath.

"Vell . . . *sure*, Russel! Dat vould be just fine vit me!" She couldn't take her eyes off the leaves. "Vould you like me to meet you somevere? You know vat I mean?"

Russ didn't hesitate this time. "Heck, no. I'll just pick you up, about five or so. Your house is that one, the second one to the east of the Zion Church, right? The one with that nice sugar maple tree out there in front, if I recall?"

CHAPTER 15
CHANCES

You'd better watch out there, Russel . . ." Elmer clicked the side of his mouth and shook his head feigning gloom. He wanted to dramatize a certain foreboding, but the crinkled corners of his eyes gave away an innocent teasing expected between good male friends. "Yup, you'd better watch out." He pulled the crank on the slot machine, bells sounded, lights flashed, and quarters tumbled into the bin below. He threw back his head in a hearty laugh and then plucked out a handful of quarters and began to feed them into the machine again. "Oh, boy, now I'm back in the game again!"

"I'll be darned, Elmer! You hit it that time!" Russ's face lit up as if wired to the machine. "It's a heck of a lot of fun watching those coins drop, you bet—but, Elmer, these quarter machines you play are little too rich for my blood, that's for sure. I'll just stick with the nickel machines . . . although, I sure didn't have your kind of luck with them today, no sir." Russ had been standing behind Elmer to watch as he finished his game, and it was during that time when Elmer had informed him of the big news in town—that Russ had been seen with Agnes Ziegenhagen at the Steak & Cake in New Ulm last Friday night. That's what prompted Elmer's warning.

"It's not luck, Russel. It's a knack for *timing*, that's what it is—knowing just when to throw in another quarter and when not." He snapped the crank again. "I'll just throw in a couple more bucks, and then we can leave. I know you're ready to go—I can always tell when you start that whistling." Elmer chuckled but his eyes didn't stray from the screen as he watched the numbers popping up.

Russ kept right on whistling, resting back on his heels as he watched the numbers too.

"But this time, Russel, I'll do just like you and *stop* while I'm ahead, hee-hee. Won't be easy to do though . . ." He glanced down at the bin of money, then back to the screen, his eyes alive and daring. "Must be at least a couple hundred in there from that Lucky 7, don't you think?" *Ca-ching . . . ca-ching . . .*

"Oh, at least that much, I'd say." Russ eyed the contents of the bin but then turned his attention to locating the other two, Hubert and Donnie. After checking his watch, he was anxious now to get the Gang rounded up and headed for home in time to make a phone call before the day slipped away. He stood tall to survey the expansive windowless room filled with rows of slot machines. The air was thick with cigarette smoke that seemed to curl from the machines themselves and then hung in a blue cloud above with the effect of a Bogart film. Except this wasn't Hollywood—this casino was in the middle of Minnesota cornfields.

Russ looked again around the room for any sign of Hubert and Donnie. Wilbur, on the other hand, would be waiting in the lobby. That's where he liked to park himself, content to people-watch while his cohorts were occupied with the games. Wilbur would be the first to admit that his buddies were lucky *not* to be under the watchful eyes of the Methodist Church like he was—so they could enjoy an hour of chance with the nickel and quarter machines at the Indian casino that afternoon.

"There they are, just coming out of the can looks like and headed this direction." Russ motioned down the aisle of machines to catch their eye. He didn't want another miscue like last month when those two ended up calling security—they couldn't find Russ and Elmer who, it turns out, weren't even *in* the casino but *outside* in the parking lot searching for the car. "Hell of an embarrassing thing," Russ muttered over and over all the way back home that day, ". . . getting security to track us down like lost kids, when just waiting another minute or two would have solved the whole danged issue!"

Now watching them meander, he reached his arm high and motioned with a loud, "Here!" Across the tops of the machines he saw Hubert's startled face, then his wave back. Russ waved and nodded, then began whistling again as he waited, keeping an eye out to make sure the two didn't get side-tracked again.

He was keeping an eye too on Elmer's last pulls of the crank. Now realizing he had only a minute or so to talk with Elmer in private, he stopped whistling and edged in front of Elmer so he could look him straight-on. "And about what you were saying awhile ago, Elmer, you know, about the Cake & Steak—you know, about Agnes Ziegenhagen?"

Elmer stayed focused on the machine, but his eyes twitched. "Yeah, what?"

"Well, I'll tell you what, Elmer—she's a darned nice person, and . . . well . . . I'll leave it at that! Hell, let them talk!" Russ surprised even himself at this dare.

At that, Elmer stopped his playing long enough to look up at Russ over his glasses with a raised eyebrow. Then, with that look of foreboding again, he turned back to his machine and pulled the crank. "Well, they're going to talk, that's for sure. Yeah, Russel, my friend, you'd better watch out." He clicked the corner of his mouth and grinned at the screen, even though that last crank didn't produce a match.

Russ unclenched his jaw and put his hands in his pockets as he looked over the machines again for the progress of the other two. He leaned back close to Elmer's ear. "Well, I can see from your attitude that you're not going to be a whole hell of a lot of help keeping the gossip down, that's for sure!" Russ resumed his whistling.

The four eventually wound their way through the network of machines to find Wilbur. But just before reaching the lobby, Russ eyed a row of quarter machines and in particular, one machine that he noticed had been recently vacated. The young man stepping away from it was muttering to himself as he slapped his cap against his jeans. Russ stopped. "Hold on just a minute there, boys. Hold on just a minute." Elmer, Hubert, and Donnie turned and watched as he fished in his pocket. "I've got a notion here about this lonely quarter in my pocket." He held out the quarter for all to see like a magician at a carnival. "I figure since I just came out *even* today, I might as well give this one, lonely quarter a try. Yes, sir, let's see what happens. It's probably a lucky quarter in fact, and this here looks like a lucky machine. Yup, the Red, White and Blue Stars and Stripes—that's lucky for sure."

"Okay, okay, Russel, you go for it, but remember—you're our driver so you can't be gambling *all* night . . ." Elmer winked, and the three snickered and rolled their eyes as Russ inserted the quarter and pulled the crank. Russ's smile was smug and confident as the machine whirred. Then flags began to appear: one . . . two . . . then straight across. All flags! "H-o-l-y buckets! What did I tell you!" He zipped his jacket with a certain flair as the coins spilled out of the machine. "Now *that* was good timing!" he said to the couple at the next machine, caught up with the big win, their eyes wide. The other three stood with mouths open, and Russ especially looked at Elmer.

Elmer nodded with a smile. "Good timing."

But Russ didn't feel particularly lucky or a good sense of timing the Friday night before, when he drove Agnes home after his pay-back meal at the Cake & Steak in New Ulm. That's what it was after all, he told himself, after the daughter's convincing argument: "Dad, just think of it as doing something nice to pay back a nice deed." Russ didn't have any other intentions really—just get it done, he thought, "pay-back."

He certainly didn't want to throw a wrench in the Gang's activities because, after all, they relied on him. He was the driver. Then there was the less generous motive: the Gang was good back-up for meals. *That* he didn't want to screw up. Rich's warning from his dying bed hung over him like a stalled winter storm—the warning about eating alone, day after day, on and on, staring at the clock. Then after some months or even years of that, something along the lines of Meals-on-Wheels might be the only alternative—that's if a guy might not be up to boiling some spuds on his own. This was Rich's dark forecast. But then, Russ had quickly pointed out, at least with Meals-on-Wheels, a guy could have a conversation with the person who would be delivering the grub—a consideration anyway. To that flimsy argument, Rich, even in his weakened state and with a look of alarm, exclaimed, "For heaven's sakes, Russel!" Well, the point was, these scenarios, along with the scary final one—the nursing home—would be inevitable if he just up and quit the chauffeur role. Rich knew how to get to Russ. So, no, he wasn't going to draw a line in the sand like that with the Gang.

On the other hand, spending an hour or so over supper with someone who just happened to be of the female gender and who just happened to share some of his interests, well, that might be a welcome change from the old duffers who seemed to like nothing better these days than an entire evening haggling about the price of soy beans or, worse, comparing ailments—not that Russ didn't have his own. He would be the first to admit he wasn't getting any younger. He just didn't need to compare notes about it. Something Oprah said the other day sounded like an attitude he'd prefer instead—about keeping an open mind to all people and all possibilities—that made perfect sense. Oprah had some pretty good lessons for people staying young.

So this was his rational as he sat in the car with Agnes in her driveway that Friday night when the question of good luck or a sense of timing could be argued. They were finishing a conversation which had started about fifteen minutes earlier as they drove past the fields coming back into town. She was noting the bumper crop of sugar beets. From there, the conversation meandered, as conversations often do, to the change in farming and women's roles on the farm, then to the additional hiring of women at the sugar beet plant near Redwood Falls, and then, to Oprah's recent show on inappropriate behavior at the workplace and the troubles at the Illinois meat packing plant. Russ had piped up, "That's what those lawyers call 'sexual harassment,' I understand."

"Yeah, yeah, that's vhat they call it. Sexual harassment—you know, it's vhen men put their hands vere they shouldn't, vhen they're supposed to be doing deir work!" Agnes seemed confident of her knowledge of the subject. She had straightened up in her seat.

Russ was up on the news, and the Oprah show too for that matter, so he enjoyed this deeper sort of topic which would circle around to where he liked to give his opinion—on what was wrong with the world these days: lawyers. "Yeah, and then these guys can get into a whole gol darn bunch of trouble, sounds like it, when the gals start complaining to lawyers. Now don't get me wrong—of course, I agree one hundred percent, it's not right touching around where a guy isn't supposed to—but it's the damned lawyers that get the most out of it. That's what gets me! Lawyers!"

Agnes was looking straight ahead now with her hands folded on her lap, and she didn't appear to be as engaged in the matter now, at least not in the facts. With the fading light of the evening sky gentle on her face, she had the appearance of a timid school girl on prom night, though her thoughts were far more seductive than that. After the call from Russ the day before, she had a romantic scenario in mind, and now, with this sizzling topic presenting itself just out of the blue, a topic even including the word "sexual," she knew it was the perfect lead-in. She sighed and in a breathy voice said, "I'll tell you vhat, Russel: You can touch me *anyvhere* . . . and I von't make a complaint!" She said it with conviction, the way a heroine might take a stand. Even Oprah might raise an eyebrow on this one, Russ thought much later when he reviewed the events of the evening from a safe distance, in his easy chair. For now, well, it was quite enough to startle him enough that he dropped his jaw—and his keys, which he had been fiddling with since turning off the car. Agnes remained seated as she was, just looking straight ahead as if she had declared this to the windshield.

What the hell? What was that she just said? This is what was screaming in Russ's ears as he scrambled to stop the keys from falling. He was glad for the diversion with the keys so he could collect his senses. But the keys landed precariously near Agnes's foot, and as he picked them up, her foot nudged closer. With that, he bounced up, just nicking his head on the dashboard and at the same time brushing her knee with the side of his hand. "Oops." He cleared his throat as he returned the keys to the ignition, and she remained looking ahead, except with a modest smile.

Russ smoothed back his hair and turned up his hearing aid, as if waiting for the right words to come to him through the hearing device. Mercifully, a laugh erupted instead. It was from high in his chest where he felt particularly constricted, but just the same, it was a polite, well-meaning laugh, the kind of laugh to acknowledge another's attempt at a joke. "Oh, yeah, that's a good one, Agnes, I'll keep that in mind. Yeah, that's a good one." His laugh simmered to a chuckle half under his breath—it worked really well to fill in the awkward space now surrounding the two. With no outward response from Agnes, he reach over to pat her hand, to acknowledge the good joke of course, much like guys slap each other on the back. But only a quick, light pat, and then he returned his hand to the steering wheel where he held on tight.

Agnes turned to look him in the eye, but she wasn't laughing. Instead, she smiled the sort of sensual smile that Russ would later relate—again at that safe distance in his easy chair—to an NFL football commercial for men's razors. The difference, of course, was that she wasn't a twenty-something-year-old model. She slinked nearer to him in a swift move across the car seat, smooth and effortless it seemed, bringing her face up close to his along with that smell of the outdoors mixed with perfume again. "I'm *not* joking, Russel!" Her German accent snapped. "You are a very nice man, and I vould be happy to spend more time vith you, doing the tings you like to do, the voods, the fishing, the valley. I can *cook* for you next time—you don't need all dose restaurants vith the guys. They don't even appreciate you. I'll even drive!" Immersed in the thrill of dramatics, somehow she still knew her limits with this man so naïve and inexperienced, so frightened really, that his hands remained clutched white-knuckled to the steering wheel. So she stopped there. Besides, she told herself, dangling a carrot or two might just do the trick. She squeezed his hand. Then with a similar sweep back across the seat, she turned to open her door. "Tank you very much for such a lovely time, Russel!"

Still with some of his wits about him, Russ grabbed for his door handle to properly escort her, but she shushed a no, "Don't you get out now, Russel. See, here, I'm right at my back door, and I left the outside light on." Out of the car she hopped and then swirled down to wave a goodbye through the open door. "Bye-bye!"

This command of vitality and self-assurance that Russ was witnessing first hand, he knew without a doubt, had to be unprecedented for any woman in later years. He'd put her right up there with any of those young women on *Oprah* talking about what they called "empowered women"! This concept now was becoming crystal clear to him. "Holy Cow!" is what his head was saying, but what came out was, "Ah . . . okay then . . . yeah, I had a good time too . . . and good night now . . . watch your step . . ." He smiled and managed a weak wave across the seat just as the door closed.

Russ watched as Agnes opened the door to her house and waved to him again as a signal to leave. He turned the ignition. The sound of the motor, he was pleasantly surprised, had a reassuring hum about it, as a solid announcement of his exit to safer territory. Now with the accelerator comfortably under his foot again, he backed out of the driveway, but in a bit of haste, just brushing the peony bushes edging the sidewalk. He paused to look back at the house, seeing Agnes through her front window as she turned on the lights and pulled the drapes. "Now what the hell am I going to do about this?" he muttered out loud, pushing back his cap to scratch his head. He put the car in drive and headed for home, rolling down his window to feel the cool October air.

So, with a couple of days to ponder the situation from a safe distance and now driving home from the casino with that lucky money in his pocket, Russ couldn't help but wonder what fate might bring him if he were to put his bets on, say, a female relationship. Now that the word was out and he had his say with Elmer—which no doubt would find its way to the grapevine, or at least he hoped it would—Russ felt the urge to tempt whatever his lot, just to bait the Morgan busybodies. The only problem was: this kind of thinking seemed to be just one end of a pendulum—on the other end was sheer terror at the thought of a determined woman. And so the pendulum was swinging for Russ.

"Say, Russ, you made out pretty good with that last crank. How much was that anyway?" Donnie in the back seat was craning his neck forward to be sure he was heard over the heater fan. Usually with little to say, much less an opinion, he had a heightened interest in a winning such as this, rarely parting with his own nickels or quarters.

"A hundred eighty bucks is what it was. Heck of a deal for a quarter, yes sir . . . ah huh . . . "

"Whew!" Donnie looked over at Hubert and Wilbur next to him, both nodding in agreement with wide eyes and raised eyebrows, and then he leaned back in his seat, still fiddling with the change in his jacket pocket.

"Have to say, Russel, you hit that one right!" Elmer reached over to pat Russ' shoulder. "Me . . . well, after all that playing, I only ended up thirty bucks ahead. Sure was fun though, especially when I was a couple hundred ahead. I just love to hear those bells and whistles." He settled back in his seat content.

Hubert looked out at the passing field and the silhouetted farmstead against the twilight sky. He grumped, "Yeah, I quit when I was even, that's plenty good for me."

Wilbur with his usual prim smile was twiddling his thumbs over his lap. "Well, boys, looks like I sure missed all the excitement again. But out there in the lobby, I did see Pastor Kleinberg's daughter there with the Borgeson boy, you know the Alvin Borgesons out on the east road. Oh, I'm *sure* they were just attending the show . . ." His eyes glanced around the car for a reaction to the notion that the Missouri Synod preacher might not favor his daughter dating a Catholic, much less frequenting a place of gambling.

But Donnie, still mesmerized by Russ's win, jumped in with his own reaction. "That makes me think of your winnings just last month, Russel, you know . . . when you gave it to your church . . . is that what you're doing again?"

"Hell no!" Russ especially loved to throw in an expletive when Wilbur was in earshot. "That was a one-time deal for the new church elevator. Naw, this I'll just sock away for something special." Glad though that Donnie brought it up, he smiled to himself and half chuckled remembering the look on Reverend Woodstrom's face last spring when Russ asked if the church would accept a donation of $200 for the elevator fund—that is, accept a donation won at the *casino*. Of course, after a serious pause and throat-clearing, Reverend Woodstrom accepted it, and Russ walked away satisfied with one-upping the prim and proper notions of the church. "Yeah, I loved the look on the Reverend's face when I said *casino*. Got him to thinking how much he wanted that money, gol darn it." The others smiled in wonder. "But this time, Donnie . . . no, I have in mind maybe something special . . . like a trip fund."

From the nods all around, that sounded reasonable, and they waited for Russ to say more. But he didn't. Each then was prompted to mull his own idea of what sort of trip that might be and if they might be included in Russ's plans. A quiet chorus of "Hmm" filled the car. But then a pheasant flitted across the highway, causing Russ to break suddenly, and then the chatter turned to the demise of pheasants from sprayed ditches, the stages of harvested corn and bean fields there along the country road, and the cooler weather blowing in from the northwest. The trip fund didn't come up again. And, with the conversation so easy and comfortable, Russ half forgot his hurry to get home, choosing to take a longer route past the historic Gilfillan Estate to round out the trip.

As they made their usual pass through Vernon Avenue to size up any activity there before calling it a night, a group of ladies was leaving the Morgan Café. Apparently, it was one those women's groups starting to show up there about once a month. Russ breathed a sigh of relief when he didn't see Agnes in the group. But it was enough of a distraction that he almost missed the stop sign so he had to put the brakes to the floor when he noticed it. "Cripes sake, Russel!" Elmer had to brace himself on the dashboard, and the three in the back all lurched forward pushing against the front seat. Elmer did a sheepish wave to the ladies who had stopped to take notice, then turned with a sly grin to face Russ. In that same devilish tone from earlier in the evening, he jibed, "You'd better watch out there, Russel. Just keep your eyes on the road. Yeah, you'd better watch out . . ."

That was quite enough to jolt Russ back to that other end of the pendulum again. "Gosh, darn, I'm slipping up here . . . " Annoyed at himself for the careless driving, he stepped on the gas unusually hard which in turn threw everyone back in their normal positions. The car sped off in silence in the direction of Elmer's farm.

Then, Wilbur began to giggle. "You're driving like *I* drive, Russel!" Russ could see in the rear-view mirror that reserved Wilbur was beside himself with his hand up against his lips, containing his amusement, even bringing up his own shortcomings. Wilbur's erratic driving, and what should be done about it, had only been discussed *outside* his presence—until now, that is.

Elmer turned to the back seat with an exaggerated wail, "Oh, no, not Russel too . . . !" One by one around the car, the giggles started. Russ finally joined in.

So it was that the Gang could claim good luck and timing that particular night. Elmer saw to it. He even announced that his son Norman would be making a beef brisket with all the trimmings that next Sunday afternoon during the World Series, and everyone was invited. "How does that sound?" He cocked his head and eyed Russ especially before closing the car door.

"Sounds good to me, Elmer—count me in."

"Well, okay then." Elmer winked and lumbered off to his house.

Russ stashed his lucky money first thing when he walked into the house—he slid the bills into a crisp business envelope marked "TRIP" in bold letters, and tucked it away in his desk drawer in the basement. "There!" Sitting at the desk, he looked at the telephone, remembering the call he planned to make. But as he reached for the receiver, his eyes fell on an old photo he had tacked on his peg board a couple years back. A waitress had taken the photo of the Gang at one of the birthdays, he couldn't remember whose, but Rich was there, and Roy. All had their glasses raised in a toast. He sighed long, with his hand on the telephone, still gazing into that snapshot. "Straightening the photo, he busied himself sorting and rearranging the clippings and other photos with the Gang."

Some time later, Russ settled into his recliner and turned the channel to a re-run of the *Lawrence Welk Show*, Lorraine's favorite.

CHAPTER 16
WILD BLUE YONDER

aybe Elmer was right that it's all about the timing. Elmer certainly knew just the time and place to throw in a trump card on that Sunday afternoon in the fall when his sons served up that beef brisket dinner with all the trimmings, even mixing in some baseball. Whether it was Elmer's doing or just plain good luck for the guys, Russ welcomed the diversion after that talk with Agnes in her driveway—that talk which had him nearly running over the peony bushes on his fast exit that night. In his most private thoughts, Russ referred to it as the "touch-me-anywhere" conversation, and it replayed like a stuck record. Anyone knows that diversions are good for a condition like this.

Elmer's generous invitation seemed to set off a series of generous happenings with the guys, now all on their good behavior, apparently in-the-know about Russ's new option for social engagements. For them, that new option, of course, would mean losing their driver. No wheels. So when Hubert celebrated his eighty-fifth birthday, just a week after the beef brisket dinner at Elmer's house, he surprised the guys with a round of drinks, and at the end of the meal a scoop of ice cream to boot. This was at the Food Shed where Hubert's granddaughter happened to be waitressing that night—so it was that she too was a recipient of the new attitude in giving since her tip of $1.25 was by far the most in Gang history. Then, about a week later after a night out at the Klostner Supper Club, some forty miles away and one of their longer drives, Donnie and Wilbur, both well-known for their tight-fistedness, each handed Russ a couple bucks for gas. Donnie's motive could have been in question because it was that same night when he announced on the drive home, "Well, I won't be here ten years from now—I'll be gone." This was after a long discussion on health issues and the unfortunate passing of Roy, then Rich, and then Donnie's own reliance on multiple medications for a heart condition, as well as depression. So his generosity might just have been guilt when facing his own demise. No matter, Russ gladly tucked the bills in his shirt pocket and chalked it up to a little nudge from the Good Lord Almighty, a god of plenty. The whole general attitude had changed, it seemed.

The early winter months provided Russ with more welcome diversions. And like a dividend, the abundance of activities kept him well-fed too. There was the trip with the daughters to commemorate World War II vets, which on its own was more than a guy could ever expect for a good time with lots of eats—the added bonus, the way he saw it, was that the event was three hundred miles away, placing him at a comfortable distance from lady-friend concerns. And, of course, the usual holiday events filled Russ' calendar and stomach nicely—the family get-togethers, the civic gatherings, and the much-anticipated employee holiday party at the gas station, with the boss serving up everything from shrimp cocktail to steak-on-skewers.

Then January, though a bleak month to most, for Russ was a welcome time of indoor organizing and waiting-out the bitter cold by focusing on seed catalogues and inspirations for spring planting. In early February, those inspirations even spurred Russ to cook again for the guys. Eager to clear out his root cellar and freezer, he served up a hearty meal of potatoes and carrots with a couple of roast ducks that he had bagged at the Thorwald slough back in October.

But that meal did more than clear out Russ's root cellar and freezer—it seemed to clear his head from some of the discontent that had been gnawing. The comfort and ease of talking with his predictable friends as they sat around the table that predictable evening caught him off guard. This he hadn't figured on. "Darned nice getting together," he thought. Was it the brandy, he wondered. Even when the conversation dragged on and on about the usual age-related ailments, followed logically by an exchange on recent obituaries—even when Hubert boasted for the umpteenth time that the nursing home was sitting on land he once owned and would soon be home to *all* of them there at the table, a forecast that brightened only *his* face—even when Wilbur repeated himself for the fourth time that evening with the news that his daughter was begging him to live with her family in Milwaukee—and even when young Donnie, in his infinite gloom interrupted, "Well, I'm still alive—but them golden years, they aren't that great"—*even then*, Russ felt an affectionate tug for these guys. Whether or not brandy was in the equation, he recognized that winter in Minnesota can do this to conversations, regardless of age. And he reminded himself that his own health could stand improvement, what with that breathing issue not getting any better.

"Let's toast to an early spring!" he said as he brought out a second bottle of apricot bandy. Elmer scrambled to raise his glass, "Now that's the spirit, Russel! To an early spring—and to the old Gang! We've been together nearly nine years!"

"To the Gang!" Elmer led the group.

The others grabbed their glasses too in the hearty toast, and Russ felt a rush of pride with the warm brandy going down. Nine years!

But spring wasn't early that year, which, of course, offered up even more time for soul-searching or, at least, weighing options. The usual late-March blizzard roared across the Midwest and shut down the Morgan community for two days until additional road crews from neighboring Franklin were called in to assist with snow removal. The snow banks at intersections were so deep that car antennas were tied with orange ribbons to give notice high above the snow to approaching drivers. The snow and chilly temperatures lingered on into April. Meanwhile, Russ's tomato seedlings, which in his eagerness he had started even earlier than other springs, were leggy and awkward-looking as if in clothes too small, as they turned to the faint sun each day in their little peat pots on the front porch.

Then one day in late April, like someone had flipped a switch, it was spring and everybody knew for certain they could pack away their winter coats. Russ's phone rang as usual around four o'clock that Sunday afternoon, "Yeah, Russel, aren't you getting hungry?" It was Elmer in his role as co-organizer which he had taken on with great gusto ever since the situation with Agnes last fall. He knew staying one step ahead was crucial. "I hear that the Truck Stop Café in Clements is open now on Sundays—want to give that place a try? Or, we can always get our calico soup in Redwood—I know that's your favorite, Russel."

"Are you sure that place in Clements is open? Seems like I've heard that before . . ."

"It says so according to an ad in the *Redwood Gazette* this week. Got it right here—'now open Sundays, eleven to nine.' That's what it says right here."

"Well, suppose we could take a little drive to Clements and find out for ourselves. Why don't you check with the others and let me know who to pick up. I'd want to leave here pretty darn soon so we have plenty of daylight—I'd like to see how the fields are shaping up after all the flooding."

"Okay! I'll get right back to you . . ." Elmer's words faded in his hurry to hang up the phone and then get back on it to the other three who had called him twice already that afternoon. Plus, he had in mind to invite Clarence Zelk who lost his wife over the winter—actually "lost" her to the nursing home where now she shared a small room with a bedridden woman, half out of her mind yelling obscenities to the aides. Clarence's wife, they said, had quit talking. She preferred now to sit for hours in her wheelchair by the big front window in the dining room, looking out into the cornfields—her eyes faraway. Clarence had been sitting in on card games recently at the pool hall. Wouldn't hurt, Elmer figured, to mix in some new blood. He knew that Russ would go for that.

Thanks to Elmer's stepping-up, the Gang had hung together over the winter, even with snow storms and icy roads, opting for shorter trips and staying close to home. Local events, like the Methodist chow mein supper and the VFW bingo-buffalo-burger feed were handy alternatives in the dead of winter. And even through the crippling flu season, when one or two were laid up for a week at a time, the Ford Taurus picked up the others for a supper out. So now, on this mild spring evening, the crowded Taurus sped down the dry pavement in abandon, the riders half convinced they had just been let out of school. And that's the effect of spring in Minnesota, regardless of age.

Baseball has that effect too. Elmer's face was flushed with excitement when he offered up his idea that evening, "Listen up, guys— now that we're all here . . . you too, Clarence . . ." He leaned his head back so that all in the car could hear, and he talked extra loud to be heard over the open windows. "The Farmers Elevator is sponsoring a bus to the Twins opener next week. Anyone interested just tell me, and I'll get the tickets. Fifteen bucks is all it'll cost you, and that includes a pretty good seat. It's a Wednesday afternoon game."

Their eyes lit up. The reality of actually attending a game, however, for this particular group with varying conditions of bad knees and weak bladders, meant more about easy access to seating and toilets. So it was that just Russ and Donnie and Elmer took the bus that next Wednesday. Even so, the effect of that first pitch was the same for all, whether at the Metrodome or listening to 'CCO radio from an easy chair with a toilet nearby—this could be a winning season.

Agnes was listening to the Twins opener too there in her living room as she busied her hands with crocheting. The delicate miniature duck she was crafting looked in sharp contrast to her strong, gnarly hands, which moved deftly through the skein. She smiled and stomped her foot when the announcer exclaimed, "It's . . . out of the ballpark, folks! Twins win it, 7 to 6!" She had seen Russ's name on the bus sign-up sheet posted at the Morgan Café this past week so she pictured him now there at the impressive new Metrodome taking it all in, probably standing up and cheering that final homerun. This would be a good topic for conversation the next time she ran into him.

Their exchanges over the winter had been brief at best with just a passing "Hello, nice to see you," or just a nod and smile from across Vernon Avenue or a crowded church basement. Their last encounter was that awkward day last fall only a couple of weeks after that pay-back dinner at the Steak and Ale, with the accompanying touch-me-anywhere comment. That's when they happened to meet at the post office. That's when Russ kindly acknowledged Agnes's offer for supper the next night, but declined because of plans for Hubert's birthday—an honest excuse. When she pursued scheduling further, Russ felt that jab in his stomach again which seized up his throat and threw him into a coughing fit. The words he managed to get out included a "thank you very much" . . . unavailable for quite some time . . . travel plans with my daughters." Then he added as he checked his watch, ". . . need to get going." He cleared his throat a final time and seemed to have regained his composure. He brought a handkerchief out of his pocket and blew his nose. Agnes stood there wide-eyed and out of words herself for a second or two. Then letting it all sink in, she smiled and said, "Vell, I always knew you vere a busy man, Russel," and she winked. "I'll be seeing you around dhough. Vemember, you can always haf a vaincheck when you vant to haf a nice homecooked meal . . ." and she turned to get into her car, with her usual flair. "And take care of dat cough," she said as she drove away.

But that conversation was months ago—an entire winter really which was like time multiplied for a woman the age of Agnes—and certainly ample time for any man to get his wits about him. This is what Agnes thought now as she turned off the radio and set her crocheting aside. "No!" she said out loud as if responding to a visitor in the nearby armchair, "I'm not going to vait around any longer. I'll call him ven dat bus gets home tonight!" She stomped her foot again and smiled.

And she did call. Russ's phone rang a few minutes after nine o'-clock that night, just when he had settled into his recliner to wait for the evening news program. He was tired from the big event. But, like that fresh spring weather lately, the phone call was welcomed with his pent-up news about the day. Agnes's pure enthusiasm seemed to spread energy right over the phone line like a dose of pep. Russ not only replayed the hits and runs as his words tumbled out, but the entire bus trip, there and back. Agnes just listened until he had finished. "I'm glad you had such a goot time, Russel. Vell, it's getting late, so I'll let you go now. Good night, now."

"Ah . . . yeah, and good night to you too, Agnes." The phone clicked on the other end almost before Russ had his words out. "Gosh darn," he wondered out loud, "that sure was out of the blue . . . and she sure didn't say much . . . ?"

As she got ready for bed, Agnes hummed with a girlish glee the tune stuck in her head since the seventh inning stretch, "Take me out to the ball game . . ." She chuckled to herself thinking of Russ's replay of the old couple sitting next to him at the stadium, heavy set, wearing matching Twins shirts, and sharing the biggest box of popcorn he'd ever seen. She liked that about Russ—he had good stories. She could be patient for a little longer.

It was just after the Honor Guard had fired their salute and the high school band trumpet player finished "Taps" that Agnes nudged her way through the small crowd to stand next to Russ at the city cemetery on the windy hill just a mile out of town. Russ appeared to be by himself this Memorial Day. Standing tall as he saluted the flag, he was a soldier again, oblivious to all else. Just as he lowered his arm, he noticed her standing next to him. He just smiled and nodded his head in a greeting while the chaplain concluded the ceremony. Agnes whispered, "Hello, Russel," and then she bowed her head to the benediction. A picnic, that's what was on her mind though, and she offered up her little prayer about that possibility.

And a picnic it turned out to be that lovely May holiday with a temperate breeze just enough for a sweater and the sky an intense blue with an occasional puffy cloud. Timing was everything that day when Agnes offered Russ the idea as the crowd dispersed from the ceremony and she walked with him to his car. "A picnic? Hmm . . . in the valley, you say? Hmm . . . well, I sure don't have anything else going on. Thought a daughter might be here today, but something else came up. And the guys, well, none of them are vets, so they're not here to give their two cents. Hmm . . . I suppose a guy couldn't get a better day than this for a picnic, that's for sure." Russ looked at the sky to confirm his decision. "Well, sure, Agnes!" He smiled back at her, relaxed now with his hands in his pockets and waiting to hear how this might happen. "But, wait a minute . . ." He cocked his head to reconsider. ". . . The stores around here aren't open today, and I'm not sure what I have around the house to bring. A can of peaches, I know I have that . . ."

"Don't you vorry about a ting, Russel." She grabbed his arm. "I'll make up a basket in no time. And I'll pick you up—how about in an hour?" Her face was a huge smile. "And bring your fishing pole . . ." Like the clock was running, Agnes turned mid-sentence to hurry to her car, waving back at Russ. She almost bumped into a couple of the band members jostling around in fun on their way back to the bus after too-long standing at attention on this beautiful spring day. At that moment, she felt like one of them.

"Yeah, my fishing pole . . . okay," he hollered after her.

The cold fried chicken, German sour potato salad, carrot sticks, olives, pickles, a thermos of coffee, and even a couple slices of apple pie, Russ knew for sure must have been in the works long before the ceremony that morning—she didn't just *happen* to have this stuff around, he told himself, no way. But it didn't really matter. He looked at the spread, laid out picture-perfect on the picnic table covered with a red checkered cloth and complete with a centerpiece—a small U.S. flag. He was reminded of the photos in his recent *AAA* magazine featuring the pleasure of road trips on America's byways. Setting his can of peaches on the table, he said with a snicker, "Looks like maybe we'll use the peaches another time."

That was the food. As if that wasn't quite enough to befuddle poor Russ, Agnes cinched it when she brought out her fishing gear, complete with crawlers from her own backyard. With the savvy know-how of a backwoods fishing guide and the charm of a madam sorcerer, she rigged and adjusted her line, pulled a long worm out of the coffee can and swirled it through the hook twice, wiped her fingers on a cloth pinned conveniently to her pants pocket, then cast the line out far, in a low, smooth arc to the middle of the river just before the break in the riffles—a walleye spot. "Yeah, dat's goot," Russ heard her say to herself. She pulled up her tackle box for a stool on the muddy bank, sat down, and pulled her straw hat down to shield her face from the sun. In only a few minutes, she said in a hushed voice, "I tink I have bite, Russel . . ."

The picnic was the start of a new regimen for Russ, juggling between the guys and "Ag," as she liked to be called now. By early June everyone in town knew about "the new couple," and Russ was surprised that it didn't bother him in the least. "Heck," he told Ag when she quizzed him on the subject those first outings, "I don't give a darn what people think, besides, it gives them something to talk about! The way I see it, none of us is getting any younger."

Then she'd agree with a shy nod and grin. "Vell, okay den, Russel."

As for the guys, Russ promised himself do his best to hold up that end of the bargain. "A couple nights out a week for some supper and a little drive—who the heck can complain about that?" That's what Russ told the daughters, who like everyone else wondered just how much socializing a man his age could handle. Gone nearly every night, he was rarely available when they phoned. Dialing every fifteen minutes until he finally picked up, they were half crazy with worry that perhaps he was there all along, overcome with any of the dire old-age afflictions, there alone in his house. How would they feel then? And they worried about losing the safety net of the Gang. The old guys after all had watched out for each other all these years. An aggressive woman such as this Agnes might have less than noble motives, they feared. "She could leave him high and dry—you never know about these things," was what they said to each other as they compared notes. Then when they hinted at that notion to their dad, he just came back with, "Naw, Ag's a good old gal" and dropped the subject.

But Elmer didn't just hint around—the whole thing rankled him, the principle of it, a woman messing up the whole works. He spoke up every chance he got. "Now why would you want to go and do that? Tell me that, Russel!" That's what he usually said when Russ mentioned he would be busy with Ag on a particular night when he otherwise might be planning an outing with the guys. "For heaven's sake, Russel, you were married all those years—you've done that!"

Russ just shrugged it off, just like with his daughters. "Don't you worry, Elmer," Russ would just laugh, "I'm just learning what Oprah makes all the fuss about—you know, being single." But the question did hang in the back of his mind, like a nagging hall monitor: Why *would* he do that?

As for Hubert and Donnie and Wilbur, well, they kept quiet about it for the most part, hoping to keep the boat on an even keel—or car, that is. But among themselves, every day they wondered.

"Have you heard anything?" Hubert would call Elmer just as suppertime was approaching on a day which might have been part of the guys' normal routine.

"Nope."

"*Well-l-l* . . . ?" That's how it was—the uncertainty, the speculations, the undercurrent of a possible rift—with a woman in the mix. But as stoic, old, Midwest farmers do facing a dilemma such as this, when perhaps someone less self-controlled might be weakened in spirit, they instead blurt out an emphatic "Humph!" and then they carried on. In this case, that meant making use of the local resources which, of course, meant no need for long drives out of town—they actually started their cars again.

Self-starting was required too because, after all, the trip planner was occupied in places unknown. On a given night when Russ might be entertained elsewhere, Elmer and Hubert and Donnie and Wilbur might each drive to the Morgan Café which all along was so handy there on Vernon Avenue. Now in a new light, the menu looked just about perfect. Or, any of them might catch the noon meal or even a card game at Gil-Mor, though not a likely social destination but one which welcomed with open arms anyone wishing to spend even an hour with the residents, so uninspired if not unresponsive. There, Hubert even rallied as a coming-home to his beloved farm land. And there, Donnie, forever medicated on everything from anti-depressants to blood thinners, secretly found comfort knowing a nurse was on staff should he need emergency medical attention at any moment. And, if not the Morgan Café or Gil-Mor, there was always the pool hall. They made do. Still, they hoped that Russ would come to his senses.

Then Elmer died. It was a stroke that took him, but only after a tough fight, true to the good Dane he was. Russ and the other three visited him at the hospital on that nineteenth day when later the monitor registered only a flat line. He was ninety-five. That's the same day Wilbur announced on the drive home that he would be leaving the very next Sunday to stay with his daughter in Milwaukee for the winter. "She says she won't worry so much if I'm there with her," he boasted like a proud parent. The car was silent and the air heavy with each of the other men mulling his own destiny. Wilbur smiled out the window. Hubert and Donnie muttered "Humph" in unison, while Russ looked straight ahead at the road.

"How old would you be if you didn't know how old you are? Huh?" Russ posed it as a riddle even though he knew there was no pat answer. It was more like one of those puzzlers he'd read from time to time in *Reader's Digest* or heard from one of those psychologists on the Oprah Show—something that could make a person think about what's important and what isn't.

"Let's see . . . how old . . . if I didn't know how old I am?" Agnes closed her eyes to think about her answer and then just that quick she popped them open and exclaimed, "You know, Russel, I tink I vould be just getting going—you know, young!"

He smiled. "Yeah, I know what you mean, Ag." I just heard that one the other day on 'CCO—they say Carl Yastrzemski said that—you know, he's the baseball player that just retired. That's a good one though, don't you think?" He squeezed her hand and then looked out the window as the plane lifted and roared in its climb high over the city, then higher still over farmsteads and countryside. The new day's sun cast a warm glow on the snow below. Then higher, and there was just the blue sky enveloping them.

The click of the intercom signaled everyone's attention. "This is your captain, folks. We're now at our cruising altitude of 35,000 feet so I'm going to turn off the seat belt sign. I'm expecting a smooth flight so you're free to roam about the cabin. We're right on schedule for our arrival in b-e-a-u-t-i-f-u-l Hawaii! So just sit back and enjoy the ride."

Russ turned back to Ag. "Think I'll do just that," he said as he grinned and leaned back in his seat.

Epilogue

After Hubert broke his leg from a fall on the icy steps at the pool hall, he became a permanent resident at Gil-Mor Manor. He died in 2002, at age ninety-five.

Wilbur, suffering from various conditions, also took up residence at Gil-Mor. He died in 2002, age ninety-two.

Donnie continued to live on his farm and became a regular visitor each Tuesday at Gil-Mor Manor for Men's Coffee. In August 2010, he became one of the first residents at Morgan's new ten-unit assited living apartments, Gil-Mor Haven. He continues as a regular visitor for Men's Coffee.

Agnes had quadruple-bypass surgery that next spring after the Hawaii trip. Only a few months later, a stroke left her speechless and paralyzed on one side. It was Russ who found her on her kitchen floor. She lived at Gil-Mor another nine years. She died in 2006 at age ninety-five.

Six months after Agnes's stroke, Russel was hospitalized for a bleeding ulcer, a direct result of too many aspirin for his degenerated spine. He was moved to Gil-Mor as a transition to his move back home. With no alternative in Morgan then for assisted senior living, Russ lived his remaining five years there at the nursing home, just two rooms down the hall from Agnes. He pushed her wheelchair, sat with her, and helped her with her meals. Not able to say even a word, Agnes communicated with a smile and a wave of her hand. Russ didn't give up his Ford Taurus until after he had at least one more occasion to take Ag for a ride to the valley. Russ died in 2004, at age ninety-three after complications with emphysema. Agnes attended his funeral.

HOTDISH RECIPES

Potato Hotdish
Mrs. Al Hartzell
St. Michael's Favorite Recipes

2 c. diced raw potatoes
1 c. diced raw celery
2 c. peas
1 can tuna

Combine. Make a white sauce to cover. Bake 350 degrees until potatoes are done.

Kidney Bean Hotdish
Mrs. Russel Albrecht

1 lb. ground beef
½ c. chopped onion
2 c. sliced raw potatoes
1 can drained kidney beans
1 can tomato soup

Brown ground beef and onion. Mix with potatoes, beans and soup. Bake 350 degrees until potatoes are done.

About the Author

Maybe it was the twenty years as a paralegal that prepared Faye best for the pure joy of creative writing. Material too was abundant from years of her dad's stories and from her own experiences growing up in small-town-America—Morgan, Minnesota.

In 2004, Faye submitted "Russel Albrecht, The Soldier," to The Veterans History Project in Washington, D.C.—stories she compiled from her dad's narration of his experiences in Europe 1944 to 1946.

In March 2006 *Running Times Magazine* featured "Cross-Culture Running with Faye's South of the Border."

Faye has a Bachelor of Science degree from the University of Minnesota. She volunteers at Ambassador Good Samaritan Nursing Home in New Hope, Minnesota, and for Medtronic Twin Cities Marathon. She and her husband reside in Golden Valley, Minnesota, and, for three months each year, in Manzanillo, Mexico.

For more information, please visit www.fayeberger.com